TWAYNE'S WORLD AUTHORS SERIES

A Survey of the World's Literature

Sylvia E. Bowman, Indiana University

GENERAL EDITOR

SPAIN

Gerald Wade, Vanderbilt University

EDITOR

Pedro Salinas

(TWAS 283)

TWAYNE'S WORLD AUTHORS SERIES (TWAS)

The purpose of TWAS is to survey the major writers —novelists, dramatists, historians, poets, philosophers, and critics—of the nations of the world. Among the national literatures covered are those of Australia, Canada, China, Eastern Europe, France, Germany, Greece, India, Italy, Japan, Latin America, the Netherlands, New Zealand, Poland, Russia, Scandinavia, Spain, and the African nations, as well as Hebrew, Yiddish, and Latin Classical literatures. This survey is complemented by Twayne's United States Authors Series and English Authors Series.

The intent of each volume in these series is to present a critical-analytical study of the works of the writer; to include biographical and historical material that may be necessary for understanding, appreciation, and critical appraisal of the writer; and to present all material in clear, concise English—but not to vitiate the scholarly content of the work by doing so.

Pedro Salinas

By JOHN CRISPIN
Vanderbilt University

Twayne Publishers, Inc.   ::   New York

Library of Congress Cataloging in Publication Data

Crispin, John.
  Pedro Salinas.

  (Twayne's world author series, TWAS 283. Spain)
  Bibliography: p.
  1. Salinas, Pedro, 1891-1951.
PQ6635.A32Z66   861'.6'2   73-17149
  ISBN 0-8057-2784-1

MANUFACTURED IN THE UNITED STATES OF AMERICA

POUR MAMAN

Preface

Pedro Salinas belongs to a group of writers generally known as the Generation of 1927, whose activity, in the 1920's and 1930's, marked the culmination of a particularly rich period for Spanish poetry; one initiated at the turn of the century with the Modernist movement, and also including such towering figures as Antonio Machado and Juan Ramón Jiménez. The group assimilated the experiments of the various European "isms" which flourished before and after the First World War, and at the same time found inspiration in traditional Spanish ballads and folk lyrics, as well as in Spanish classical poetry of the sixteenth and seventeenth centuries. This combination of the old and the new was a unique phenomenon, since most of the parallel movements in Europe tended to reject the past almost entirely. The resulting product was highly original, and one can say in retrospect that this poetry was possibly the most significant, both quantitatively and qualitatively, to come out of the great Vanguardist adventure of the period between the two world wars.

The Generation of 1927's collective activity ended abruptly with the Spanish Civil War which caused the death of its best-known member, Federico García Lorca, and sent all but three of the remainder into exile. After 1936, each poet more or less developed in his own way. Although a general drift toward social themes can be detected in the poetry of many former members of the group, it can be attributed to the widespread reaction to the trauma and consequences of the Second World War rather than to more specific influences or group characteristics.

Salinas published his first book of poetry in 1924, and his last appeared posthumously in 1954. His work is of great interest at every stage. Early verse contains perfect illustrations of the mixture of Vanguardist experimentation with tradition which characterized the first phase of the Generation of 1927, while poetry written between 1931 and 1936—often judged his best—exemplifies the neo-Romantic revival which dominated its second phase. Some of the late poetry written in exile in the United States is particularly relevant to us since it contains warnings about various aspects of the disintegration of culture in contemporary life, and show a poet's reaction to problems which have magnified since the time when Salinas first confronted them in his new American environment, more than thirty years ago. Although Salinas' world reputation is well established, since at least ten book-length studies have already been written on his poetry in Spanish and four other major languages, the present book is the first to provide a long-overdue critical introduction in English to his works, personality, and philosophy of life.

My main objective is to show Salinas' entire creative production as an integral whole, taking as a guide the poet's own stated principle that a critic's main task should always be to define a writer's primary theme, or world-vision, and that this search should begin with the determination of his basic attitude toward reality. Critics of Salinas have held widely divergent opinions on this point. He has been viewed as a Neoplatonist, a romantic Idealist, a mystic in the oriental-pantheistic tradition, and, at the other end of the spectrum, a struggling "agonist," in quest of immortality but obsessed with Nothingness. I shall take a middle view and join those critics who define Salinas' stand as one of stoic realism. The poet is fully aware of the limitations of the material world and of the impossibility of reconciling man's existence in time with his transcendental aspirations. Disillusion when confronting these limitations may at times cause him to take refuge in a private world of dreams or Platonic ideals. In the end, however, he joyfully accepts life, with love and human solidarity as his supreme values, sufficient in themselves to give meaning to man's existence.

I have dealt with Salinas' works chronologically, marking three main periods of development: early experiments, the middle cycle of love poetry, and works written in exile. Each book of verse is examined both as a structural whole and for its place in the overall perspective. Although my approach is primarily thematic, stylistic characteristics are also examined, especially in the detailed analysis of two poems from the love cycle, and one from the social poetry of the late period. The last chapter deals with nonpoetic works which reinforce and reiterate basic themes introduced in the poetry.

Most of Salinas' poetry was translated into English by Eleanor L. Turnbull during the poet's lifetime. These translations (a complete list of which appears in my bibliography) are accurate but do not in any way attempt to match the style of the originals. Salinas seldom uses rhyme, and except in his early poetry does not rely on complex imagery. He does, however, make very subtle use of rhythm and accentuation. The translations used in this book attempt the admittedly difficult task of transposing this internal music as closely as possible from one language to the other. For this purpose, some words which do not appear in the Spanish text and which reinforce—but do not alter—the meaning of the original have been added in brackets in the English translations. One translation, that of "Escorial II" (pp. 54–55), is the work of Alice J. McVan and was published in an anthology entitled *Translations from Hispanic Poets* (New York, 1938). It is used by special permission of the editor, the Hispanic Society of America. I am indebted to my wife, Ruth Katz Crispin, for all translations followed by an asterisk (*). The remaining translations are my own.

I gratefully acknowledge the permission of Doña Soledad Salinas de Marichal and of Don Jaime Salinas to quote extensively from Salinas' poetic and nonpoetic works. I wish to thank Professor Juan Marichal for his clarification of some details of Salinas' biography, and for lending me his personal copy of the rare edition of *Amor en vilo*. I am also indebted to the Graduate Research Council of Vanderbilt University for a summer grant which financed in part the research for this book.

My earnest thanks go to my typist, Mrs. Sandra Reid, for her cheerful and patient cooperation. Above all, I am grateful to my wife Ruth for her invaluable help with the manuscript and for her contributions to the translation of Salinas' poetry.

Contents

Chronology

1891   November 27: Pedro Salinas is born in Madrid. The date of his birth is often erroneously given, even on his tombstone, as 1892.

1897- Primary education at Colegio Hispano-Francés.
1903

1909   Receives secondary school diploma from the Instituto San Isidro. Enters University of Madrid.

1911   Publishes three poems entitled "Estrofas" ("Strophes") in *Prometeo* (No. 32), a publication directed by Ramón Gómez de la Serna.

1913   Receives Licentiate in Romance Philology. Translates poems by A. Samain, H. de Régnier, C. Guérin, and L. Largnier for E. Díez-Canedo's anthology entitled *La poesía francesa moderna* (*Modern French Poetry*).

1914   Accepts post as Lecturer in Spanish at the Sorbonne.

1915   Marries Margarita Bonmatí.

1916   Presents his doctoral dissertation on "The Illustrators of Don Quixote" at the University of Madrid.

1917   Returns to Spain.

1918   Earns an appointment to a university chair in Literature and is named to a post at the University of Seville.

1920- Publishes poems in *España, La Pluma, Lunes del Imparcial*.
1922   Begins his translation of Marcel Proust's *Remembrances of Things Past*.

1922- Acts as Lecturer in Spanish at Cambridge University.
1923

1924   Publishes *Presagios* (*Presages*). The date 1923 appearing on the title page of this book is erroneous. Collaborates with Juan Ramón Jiménez in *Indice* magazine and begins publishing poems and prose in José Ortega y Gasset's *Revista de Occidente*.

1925   Publishes a critical edition of the eighteenth-century Anacreontic poet Juan Meléndez Valdés, under the title *Poesías* (*Poems*).

1926   Publishes *Víspera del gozo* (*On the Eve of Joy*), a series of narrative prose sketches. Publishes a modern verse version of the *Poema de Mío Cid* (*Poem of the Cid*).

1927 Góngora's tricentennial celebration. Salinas takes part in some of the *Homenaje* ceremonies.

1928 Works as a researcher in the Center for Historical Research in Madrid, and as Director of Courses for Foreign Students at the Central School of Languages connected with this Center.

1929 Publishes *Seguro azar* (*Steadfast Chance*).

1931 Publishes *Fábula y signo* (*Fable and Sign*), and last Proust translation.

1932 Becomes director of *Indice Literario*, official publication for contemporary literature of the Center for Historical Research.

1933 At Salinas' instigation, the International Summer University is founded at Santander. Salinas is named General Secretary and retains this post until 1936. Publishes *La voz a ti debida* (*The Voice Owed to You*). A preliminary edition of this work, containing eleven poems, had first appeared the same year under the title *Amor en vilo* (*Unbound Love*).

1936 Publishes an anthology of the Renaissance mystic Fray Luis de Granada, entitled *Maravilla del mundo* (*Wonder of the World*). Publishes *Razón de amor* (*Love's Reason*). After the outbreak of the Spanish Civil War Salinas departs for the United States, where he had been invited as a visiting professor at Wellesley College.

1937 Receives D.H.C. from Middlebury College. Teaches that summer, and many summers thereafter, in the same college's language program. Delivers a series of lectures at the Johns Hopkins University. This series will later be published in English translation by the Johns Hopkins Press, under the title *Reality and the Poet in Spanish Poetry*.

1940 Accepts a permanent position as Turnbull Professor of Hispanic Literature at Johns Hopkins. He will retain this position until his death.

1941 Publishes *Literatura española siglo XX* (*Spanish Literature, Twentieth Century*), a collection of critical essays.

1942 First edition of *Poesía junta* (*Collected Poems*).

1942-1945 Visiting Professor at the University of Puerto Rico.

1946 Publishes *El contemplado* (*The Contemplated Sea*).

1947 Publishes *Jorge Manrique, o tradición y originalidad* (*Jorge Manrique, or Tradition and Originality*). Travels in Colombia, Ecuador, and Peru.

1948 Publishes *El defensor* (*The Defender*), essays on contemporary life, and *La poesía de Rubén Darío* (*The Poetry of Rubén Darío*).

1949 Visits France, Italy, and other European countries (excluding Spain). Publishes *Todo más claro y otros poemas* (*All Things Made Clearer and Other Poems*).

1950 Publishes his novel *La bomba increíble* (*The Incredible Bomb*).

1951 Publishes *El desnudo impecable y otras narraciones* (*The Impeccable Nude and Other Stories*). Premiere of his play *La fuente del arcángel* (*The Fountain of the Archangel*) at Columbia University, New York (February 16). On December 4, Pedro Salinas dies in Phillips House, Massachusetts General Hospital, after a long illness. He is buried at Santa Magdalena Cemetery, San Juan, Puerto Rico.

1952- Publication of *Teatro:* "*La cabeza de Medusa,*" "*La estratoes-*
1953   *fera,*" "*La isla del tesoro*" (*Theater:* "*The Head of Medusa,*" "*The Stratosphere,*" "*Treasure Island*"). Several commemorative issues on Salinas are published, by *Hispania, Insula, Asomante,* and the following year in *Número* (Montevideo) and *Buenos Aires Literaria.*

1955 Publication of *Confianza* (*Confidence*) and *Poesías completas* (*Complete Poems*).

1957 Publication of *Teatro completo* (*Complete Theater*), of *Volverse sombra y otros poemas* (*To Turn to Shadow, and Other Poems*), and *Amor, mundo en peligro, poema* (*Love, A World in Peril, a Poem*).

1958 Publication of *Ensayos de literatura hispánica* (*Essays on Hispanic Literature*).

1961 Publication of *La responsabilidad del escritor* (*Responsibility of the Writer*); includes various essays previously published in *The Defender,* and in periodicals.

1971 Publication of a new revised edition of *Complete Poems,* including the reconstructed manuscript of *Largo lamento* (*A Long Lament*). Commemorative issue of *Insula* (Nos. 300-301), in observance of the twentieth anniversary of the poet's death. December: Tribute to Pedro Salinas at the University of Puerto Rico, with an address by Jorge Guillén and the staging of three of Salinas' plays.

CHAPTER 1

The Spanish Vanguard 1919-1936

I *Ultraism: The First Spanish Vanguard*

THE term Vanguard has by now become firmly established to designate two decades of artistic and literary experimentation beginning in Europe around 1910, with Cubism and Futurism, and ending with Surrealism in the 1930's. In Spain this creative experiment began only after the First World War and can be divided into two phases. During a short initial period (1919-1923), a literary movement called *Ultraísmo* (Ultraism) assimilated and repeated prewar trends as they had existed mainly in France and Italy. Concentrating especially on transforming the poetic language, the Ultraists broke new grounds and prepared the way for a second Vanguard, conventionally known as the Generation of 1927, whose collective activity began in the early 1920's and lasted until the outbreak of the Spanish Civil War in 1936. A comparison of the two groups will reveal both the similarities and differences which existed between the main trends in the European Vanguard, clearly represented by the Ultraists, and the specifically Spanish contribution offered by the Generation of 1927, to which Pedro Salinas belonged.

The Ultraist movement received its first impulse from the arrival in Spain of Paris-based artists and intellectuals, in the aftermath of the First World War. Among them was a young Chilean poet, Vicente Huidobro, who had collaborated in the *Nord-Sud* review in the experiments of Poetic Cubism along with Max Jacob, Pierre Réverdy, and others. Huidobro claimed to be the founder of a new school of poetry called Creationism, which, as the term suggests, named as the primary function of poetry the fashioning of a new reality, totally independent of

17

the forms of Nature. The Creationist concept of poetry, to which I shall later return, was to become one of the few positive tenets of Ultraism.

The Ultraist group, whose principal leaders were Rafael Cansinos-Assens, Guillermo de Torre and Gerardo Diego, really had no specific creed of its own. It favored "the new" in general and characterized itself mainly by sponsoring, between 1919 and 1921, a profusion of "little magazines," all of very short life spans (*Ultra*, 1921-1922; *Grecia*, 1920; *Tableros*, 1921; *Reflector*, 1920, and others). These literary tracts spread information about the various European "isms," and published Vanguardist manifestos, along with original poetry and translations from such sensational figures as Apollinaire and Bontempelli. In this task, the Ultraists accomplished very well their avowed purpose of Europeanizing Spanish culture, putting it in touch suddenly with what had been going on in the rest of Europe for the previous ten years.

Some of the Ultraist slogans aptly reflect the debunking nature of the movement. In the first issue of *Ultra*, we find the following:

"Ultraism consists of turning the world upside down."

"Ultraism is the train that never stops. One must get on and off at full speed."

"After Ultraism, the end of the World."

"Ultraism; the only life-sustaining oxygen."[1]

The slogans betray the strong influence of Dada, but without the bitterness and despair reflected in this movement's antiliterary and antilife stand, since the full traumatic impact of the World War was not immediately perceived in nonbelligerent Spain.

The only creative efforts of the Ultraists came in poetry. Like Poetic Cubism and the various Imagist schools which had sprung up from England to Russia, Ultraist poetry was based on complex metaphors—involving synesthesia, unusual transferences of sensations, and farfetched comparisons—which sought to render all the intellectual and emotional impact of a single instant in time. Like Futurism and Cubism, it provoked new mental associations and dissociations, and, above all, the surprise effect. All that was considered ornamentation, such as rhyme, rhythm, and other auditive qualities, as well as punctuation, was eliminated. Instead, the Ultraists were fond of visual effects. They printed their verses, at times, in geometric shapes or in the form of an object, as Apollinaire had already done in his *Calligrammes.*

Like Futurism, the Ultraist movement found its inspiration in modern urban life, and the artificial world of machines. It scorned sentimentality and denounced pseudo-realism based on a so-called faithful representation of reality, as well as the decadent elegance which it found in the Modernist (neo-Parnassian) school.

In spite of its affected ironic-skeptic pose, the spirit of Ultraism was one of childish optimism, basic love of life, and love of progress inasmuch as the group believed that speed and modern technology would increase life's intensity. The movement was somewhat marked by the historical moment: the postwar escape from all serious preoccupations and responsibility that was general in all of Europe.

By around 1923, Ultraism had accomplished its pioneering mission. The role of keeping Spain in touch with the intellectual currents of Europe and the newest Vanguardist trends was taken over by more stable and prestigious publications, such as Ortega y Gasset's *Revista de Occidente* (1923-1936), and the lively and well-informed *Gaceta Literaria* (1927-1932), to mention only two which can be said to have transcended any particular movement.

It was perhaps Ultraism, as well as European literary and artistic currents up to Dada, that Ortega had in mind when he wrote his now famous essay entitled: *La deshumanización del arte* (*The Dehumanization of Art*), written in 1923. This essay has often been invoked in interpreting the whole Spanish Vanguard, and some critics have even seen in it an aesthetic formula for the then incipient Generation of 1927. In fact, Ortega was not proposing any formula, but merely centering a discussion around seven points which he believed best characterized New Art up to the time of his essay. His observations were that the New Art (1) tends toward dehumanization; (2) seeks to avoid living forms; (3) considers a work of art as art and nothing more; (4) looks upon art as a game and nothing more; (5) is essentially ironical; (6) shuns all affections and seeks the scrupulous realization of its intent; (7) is not of transcendental nature.

These seven points adequately sum up the Ultraist position, but only the first and the sixth can be said to apply even remotely to the Generation of 1927. Even these have to be qualified. If by "dehumanization" one means intellectualization of Art (reality rendered not as immediately perceived but as reinterpreted by the imaginative faculties), and a reluctance to divulge intimate personal feelings, the term, though inaccurate, may be applied to this group. The sixth point merely implies a tendency toward "purification" and strictness of form which was indeed to be one of the new generation's main characteristics.

For the rest, the poetry of the Generation of 1927 was very much concerned with human values, and whereas Ultraism stressed pure creative expansion, and strived to free the poem from any recognizable point of reference with reality, the poets of the new group insisted from the start that the relationship between reality and a writer's inner world was poetry's concern. Literature for them was never pure creation, but always communication.[2]

II *The Generation of 1927*

The group known as the Generation of 1927 includes eight or nine major poets (and a score of minor ones), the oldest being Pedro Salinas (1891-1951) and the youngest Manuel Altolaguirre (1905-1959). On the whole it was a much more intellectual group than the Ultraists. Three members, including Salinas, Jorge Guillén (1893-   ), and the poet-critic Dámaso Alonso (1898-   ), were university professors. Federico García Lorca (1898-1936) came to Madrid to study literature at the University. Luis Cernuda (1902–1963) was one of Salinas' students at the University of Seville, and Rafael Alberti (1902-   ) also studied in Madrid for a time. In fact, the *Residencia de Estudiantes* in Madrid, where Lorca and Alberti had taken up quarters (together with such figures as Salvador Dalí and Luis Buñuel) became a focal point for the activities of the group, rather than some café *tertulia* as was customary for Spanish intellectuals.[3]

This common intellectual background was perhaps the cause for the group's return to literary tradition, which included both popular and classical poetry. Lorca and Alberti found inspiration in the folk songs of Andalusia. Traditional ballads, which have been in the mainstream of Spanish literature since the fifteenth century, influenced the style of all members of the group to a degree. Renaissance Spanish poets such as Garcilaso de la Vega and San Juan de la Cruz were also avidly read and discussed. In the summer of 1927, the commemoration of the three-hundredth anniversary of the death of another Golden Age poet, Luis de Góngora, provided the occasion for the first "generational" act of solidarity. These young writers wished to rehabilitate Góngora, who was considered obscure in style, a practitioner of "art for art's sake," and at least in his best known poems—*Las soledades* (*The Solitudes*) and *Fábula de Polifemo y Galatea* (*The Fable of Polyphemus and Galatea*)—baroque in the most pejorative sense.

The demonstration in behalf of Góngora began, in typical Vanguardist fashion, with a "pilgrimage" to Seville for a series of lectures on Góngora at that city's *Ateneo* (an event financed single-handedly by the writer-bullfighter Sánchez Mejías, later immortalized in two well-known elegies by Lorca and Alberti). There Lorca read his essay on "The Poetic Image of Luis de Góngora." (Salinas, then traveling abroad, did not attend.) In Madrid a solemn requiem Mass "for the repose of Don Luis's soul" was celebrated in one of the city's most baroque churches. An invitation to attend, signed by five members of the group, including Salinas, was sent to all distinguished intellectuals and academicians, and ignored by all but one.[4] Finally, books by some of Góngora's most virulent critics, from the seventeenth century on, were burned in a public bonfire.

In a more scholarly way, the group was responsible for a revival of Góngora studies. Dámaso Alonso published an annotated edition of *The Solitudes*. Salinas and Guillén also prepared Góngora editions, but after the enthusiasm of the Góngora celebration passed, these were never published. Gerardo Diego (1896-   ), the only transfer from the Ultraist movement, prepared a Góngora anthology. There were numerous memorial tributes to Góngora, including one in the *Revista de Occidente*,

another in *La Gaceta Literaria,* and a particularly interesting
account of Góngora commemorations was given in one of the
group's own publications: *Lola.* This memorial issue was
beautifully illustrated by such artists as Picasso and Juan Gris,
and even contained a musical tribute by Manuel de Falla.

Though Góngora's influence on the poetry of the group has
been widely exaggerated (none of the poets really tried to
imitate him, except as a passing tribute),[5] the cult of Góngora
and the other Renaissance poets is important to show the
group's attitude toward culture, at a time when the rest of
Europe resolutely rejected all connection with the past. Dámaso
Alonso has said that the group "did not rebel against anything."[6]
From the standpoint of technique, this statement is correct.
Apart from the sources already mentioned, there was to some
degree influence from the French Symbolists (Mallarmé, Valéry)
and their Spanish equivalents in Modernism. The most admired
contemporary master was the post-Symbolist Juan Ramón
Jiménez. Even Antonio Machado, whose somber existential and
deeply personal poetry is diametrically opposed to that of the
Vanguard, had some influence on the Generation from the point
of view of technique.

Though many of these poets, including Salinas, preferred
free or unrhymed verse, this in no way implied a relaxation of
form. Formal discipline was always a main concern, and all at
least tried their hand at traditional stanzas (even the sonnet,
then ridiculed as a relic of the past in the rest of Europe).
Guillén and Cernuda have a preference for the *décima* (a
ten-line stanza with no more than two consecutive lines in
rhyme). Salinas frequently used seven- and eleven-syllable verse
combinations so frequent in Renaissance Spanish poems known
as *silvas.* And as I already mentioned, the ballad verse form
(octosyllabic, with stress on the seventh syllable and assonance
in alternate lines), though used for a lyric rather than
narrative purpose, was a favorite of Lorca, Alberti, and Emilio
Prados (1899-1962), as it had already been for J. R. Jiménez
and Machado.[7] In spite of this formalism, the group was still
very much a continuation of the Vanguard, forming its con-
structive phase after the iconoclastic period of the Ultraists.

At least in its initial phase (1923-1928?), the Generation

of 1927 shared the Ultraists' optimistic outlook, the feeling
that the World had to be rediscovered through modern eyes,
and a belief that the only value was the full enjoyment of Life
itself. Accordingly there was at first no philosophical concern,
no search for any absolute, nor any sociopolitical involvement
on the part of the group. Like the Ultraists, the new poets
had equal abhorrence of sentimentality, bourgeois conventions,
and rhetoric (*lo putrefacto*), and decadentism. They also shared
the Vanguard's enthusiasm for technology, sports, the cinema,
and modern city life. Though the group was less militant and
less given to writing manifestos, it continued the cult of the
metaphor, and the experiments of Ultraism are easily traceable
in the early works of Lorca and Alberti and even Salinas or
Guillén.[8]

The main difference lay in how these images were now put
to use. Metaphors were no longer cultivated in the name of
pure creation or as a mere nonsense game. The very serious
function of the poet was to add dimension and richness to one's
perception. A well-known statement by Lorca clearly illustrates
this point:

A poet must be a teacher of the five senses. . . . To be able to be
the owner of the most beautiful images, he must open doors of
communication in all of them and very often must superimpose
their sensations and even disguise their nature.[9]

This concept of poetry, first as a means of discovery and
second as communication, is shared by all other poets in the
group and is, as we shall see, a particular concern to Pedro
Salinas (though with less emphasis than Lorca on sensual
perception).

This is the reason for the Generation of 1927's cult of
Góngora. His poetry shows a real love of the concrete world
discovered through the full ranges of the senses. The life-
vision of the Generation of 1927 in its initial period is, in fact,
very similar to Góngora's. It is what Salinas would later call
the Exaltation of Reality: Joyful Life in the Present. For Jorge
Guillén and Salinas, this was to remain a lifetime attitude,
despite passing moments of crises. For most of the others

however, there was a progressive loss of optimism and the appearance of insoluble human conflicts. Love of life was no longer a sufficient value. The transitory or illusory nature of the material world became a more frequent consideration. The poets grew dissatisfied with their surrounding, as they came to deplore the dehumanizing effect of regimented urban life.

The result was an inward withdrawal in the case of some poets like Emilio Prados, Manuel Altolaguirre, and Luis Cernuda. Others felt the need to balance reality with a private world built upon the imagination. This was the great concern of Lorca. For him, to live in an immutable dream or poetic world signified happiness, and to live in reality, especially modern reality, sooner or later, destruction.

The conflict between external and inner world with its resulting relative view of reality moves J. González Muela to say that the poets of the Generation of 1927 project progressively inward, and that reality for these poets is not the world outside, but one reshaped by their dreams and ideals.[10] Many critics see this transformation in Salinas: A very materialistic idealist, González Muela calls him. As we shall later see, this is rather putting too strong an emphasis on one side of the coin. But a basic wavering between realism and escape from reality does indeed exist in this generation, especially after 1930.

For Cernuda and Alberti, this phase ended in a neo-Romantic revolt. The growing feeling of alienation also became the pretext of techniques very close to Surrealism in Alberti, Vicente Aleixandre (1898-   ), and Lorca. For Alberti, the conflict was later resolved in political engagement, but for the rest tensions increased until the outbreak of the Civil War, which utterly shattered their world. For Lorca the war brought death, for the others subsequent exile (for all except Aleixandre and Dámaso Alonso). After the war, all the members of the Generation, to varying degrees, introduced social and historical themes in their poetry. This change is particularly marked in Aleixandre, Diego and Alonso, whose book, *Hijos de la ira* (*Sons of Wrath*), 1944, is generally seen as signaling the beginning of social poetry in Spain. For Salinas, socio-historical preoccupations are evident in the poetry of *Todo más claro* (*All Things Made Clearer*), 1949, as we shall later see.

It is a mistake, however, to see, as many critics have done, a sharp division between a first period of "dilettantish" aloofness followed by a sudden conversion after the war (some see it before the war, in the late 1930's). The Generation was from the beginning concerned with human values and with presenting a particular world-vision. As Guillén has said, "the major themes of human existence—love, nature, life, death—filled the lyric and dramatic words of this Generation."[11]

In retrospect, we can see that what held the group together was first of all, as Andrew Debicki has perceptively seen, a common agreement on the function of poetry[12] as I have described it. There is also a parallel in their evolutions from initial optimism to doubt and insecurity. In the first phase, futuristic themes, plus a fusion of traditional influences with modern experiments resulted in a poetic production quite distinct from that of the rest of the European Vanguard. Thematically also, the common preoccupation with the relative nature of reality, or with related themes: appearances vs. the true essence of things; dream world vs. concrete world. The theme of Love is frequent in the generation both as supreme value (Guillén, Salinas), and ultimately as supreme illusion (Cernuda, Altolaguirre, Alberti, Lorca), or even as a potential source of destruction (Aleixandre, Lorca, Alberti). The theme of solitude, personal alienation and the corrosion of Time, fear of Nothingness, are frequently recurrent, especially after 1929—in Alberti's *Sobre los ángeles* (*Concerning the Angels*), in Cernuda, in Lorca. We shall find many of these attitudes and themes in the works of Pedro Salinas, who is perhaps the most balanced prototype of his generation.

CHAPTER 2

Teacher, Critic, and Poet

I *Pedro Salinas: Life and Personality*

PEDRO Salinas Serrano was born in Madrid on November 27, 1891. His family owned a small shop in the city's oldest and most picturesque section, in the immediate vicinity of the Plaza Mayor. Madrid was then still the near-provincial city depicted in the novels of Benito Pérez Galdós, and Salinas' early childhood corresponded with the last few years of its placid Restoration period, prior to the awakening caused by the loss of the war with the United States in 1898-1899. Salinas remembered this world with great nostalgia, and Madrid always remained the city with which he best identified. His speech never lost certain peculiarities of expression and vocabulary typical of the capital, and he possessed the dry sense of humor and ironic skepticism which is often ascribed, in novels and plays, to the "typical Madrilenian."

Young Pedro received his primary education at Madrid's Colegio Hispano-Francés, where he came in contact, at this early age, with the French language, and obtained his secondary school diploma from the Instituto San Isidro in 1909. The same year, he registered at the University of Madrid for courses in Law and Romance Philology. For three years he pursued this dual interest, but his love of literature finally prevailed, and he was graduated in 1913 with a Licentiate in Letters degree. His earliest-known poems date from those student days. Only four have survived, originally published in Ramón Gómez de la Serna's *Prometeo* review, in 1911, and reprinted only recently in the definitive edition of his *Poesías completas* (*Complete Poems*).[1] These poems, which the author later qualified as *espeluznantes* (hair-raising), show a normal adolescent Romantic bent, and a certain admiration for the Symbolist and Modernist

26

aesthetics (especially in the fourth poem, dedicated to the French poet Jean Moréas).

Upon graduation, Salinas accepted a post as lecturer in Spanish at the Sorbonne. He lived in Paris from 1914 to 1917, teaching literature, working on his doctoral dissertation on "The Illustrators of Don Quijote," and making acquaintances in the many literary and artistic circles of the Vanguard. Paul Valéry was among the prominent writers whom he met at this time, and the one he most admired. To supplement his income, he also translated into Spanish some war propaganda tracts for the allies.[2] While living in Paris, in the summer of 1915, he married Margarita Bonmatí, a girl of Spanish origins (Alicante), but whose family lived in Algiers.

Having completed his dissertation, Salinas returned to Spain, and in 1918 entered the national competition for teaching posts at the university level. He won a professorship (*cátedra*) in Spanish Literature, with choices of an assignment at the University of Murcia or that of Seville. Salinas chose the latter city. He was to remain in Seville for eight years, interrupted only by short stays in Madrid, by lecture tours, and one year spent as a visiting lecturer at Cambridge University (1922-1923). By his own admission, the years in Seville made a profound impression on him. He was captivated by the brightness and color of the Andalusian city and by its exotic beauty resulting from the confluence of the Arabic and Occidental cultures. "Entrada en Sevilla" ("Entering Seville"), one of the prose vignettes of his second published book, *Víspera del gozo* (*On the Eve of Joy*), is a testament to his admiration.

Salinas' literary activity had begun in earnest after his return from France. During the next five years, he published poems in several important newspapers and magazines (*España, La Pluma, Indice*), and in the more ephemeral reviews of the Vanguard. Some of these poems, including two important sonnets published in the supplement of a Madrid daily called *Lunes del Imparcial* (January 7, 1918), were to be incorporated in his first volume of verse in 1924. This book was entitled *Presagios* (*Presages*) and its publication was encouraged by Juan Ramón Jiménez who suggested the order of the poems and insisted on including the book among the first offerings of his select *Biblioteca de Indice.* He also wrote a preface of introduction and praise of the new poet. Another important collaboration began in 1924, with José Ortega y Gasset and his newly founded *Revista de Occidente.* Salinas became a regular contributor to the prestigious magazine. Many of his poems were published there for the first time (some of these texts offer interesting variants to the definitive versions),[3] as well as prose selections, including the aforementioned "Entering Seville." *On the Eve of Joy* was published in *Revista de Occidente*'s "*Nova Novorum*" collection, in 1926.

As Salinas spent more and more time in the literary circles of Madrid, he gave up his university chair and moved to the capital. He began associating with the other future members of the Generation of 1927, developing close friendships with several of them, even though he was somewhat older and commanded a certain respect due to his university professorship (many continued to address him as "Don Pedro"). He became particularly close to Jorge Guillén whose career was parallel to his and who, by chance, happened to succeed him in many of the posts that he left behind (at the Sorbonne, in Seville, at Cambridge, and later at Wellesley College). Years later, Salinas left a moving testimony of his friendship with most of the poets of the group in a series of reminiscences, entitled "Nueve o diez poetas" ("Nine or Ten Poets") which served as the introduction to a bilingual anthology of contemporary Spanish poetry published by the Johns Hopkins Press.[4]

From 1928 to 1936, Salinas' primary official occupation was that of researcher in the Center for Historical Studies, a government-sponsored institute under the direction of the famed medieval scholar, Ramón Menéndez Pidal. Salinas took charge of the section on modern literature. Later (1932) he founded *Indice Literario,* one of the Center's publications, devoted exclusively to criticism and reviews of contemporary currents. Some of the articles written in these pages were collected in his book entitled *Literatura española siglo XX* (Mexico, 1941). Meanwhile, he continued to gain fame as a poet. Between 1929 and 1936, he published four books of verse, including his two most famous works: *La voz a tí debida* (*The Voice Owed to You*), and *Razón de amor* (*Love's Reason*). His other publications consisted of scholarly editions, a modern verse rendition of the *Poem of the Cid*, and translations from the French, including the first three parts of Marcel Proust's *A la Recherche du Temps Perdu* (*Remembrances of Things Past*).[5] He continued teaching part-time at the University of Madrid, and served as Course Director at the Central School of Languages opened by the Center to foreign students. At his urging, the Republican government founded the International Summer University of Santander (1933-1936), one of the first European summer programs for foreign university students. Salinas served as its General Secretary, and under his leadership the program was highly successful in attracting distinguished teachers and scholars from all over the world.

Even before the outbreak of the Spanish Civil War in 1936, Salinas had made no secret of his sympathies for liberal Republicanism. Like most intellectuals, he had supported the Republic from the start, and he remained a Loyalist throughout the conflict. However, he refused to involve himself directly in politics, and he deplored sectarian fanaticism on either side. In the spring of 1936, he had accepted a visiting professorship at Wellesley College (Massachusetts), and he decided to keep his commitment in spite of the outbreak of the war in July. He left for the United States in the late summer of 1936. What was planned as no more than a temporary stay turned out to be the beginning of fifteen years of exile.

Life in exile and separation from his Hispanic culture was never easy for Salinas, although his feelings toward the United States were of deep gratitude for the hospitality accorded him, and admiration for the sincerity and cordiality of its people. He was fascinated by this country, which he looked upon as a gigantic "toyland," and he had an endless curiosity for "gadgets." He liked to walk through five-and-dime stores or to window-shop, and knew his way around New York, Boston, and other cities of the Eastern seaboard. An indefatigable traveler, he was forever on lecture jaunts from one end of the continent to the other.[6] Finally, he never ceased to praise American libraries, from the large academic institutions to the humble one-room public libraries which, to his amazement, he found even in the smallest towns. But, as we shall see in the discussion of his late works, he was frightened by the rapid advances of technology and the coming into being of a consumer mass culture which, he feared, would depersonalize and despiritualize the individual.

Salinas' years in the United States turned out to be his most productive as a man of letters. From 1940 to 1951, he published two books of poetry, his best literary criticism, and prose fiction. Additional poetry of this period, and twelve plays, were to be published posthumously. He remained at Wellesley for three years, then was honored with an appointment to a specially endowed professorship in Hispanic Literature at the Johns Hopkins University. Baltimore became his official residence and remained so until his death, although he also taught on a visiting basis at numerous American universities, from the East Coast to California. His summers were almost invariably spent at Middlebury College in Vermont, where he taught in the college's well-known summer language program.

One particularly important period in his life was a three-year stay at the University of Puerto Rico (1942-1945). These were the happiest years of his exile, since he found himself once again speaking his own language and taking part in a cultural life more like the one he had left in Spain. The poetry written in Puerto Rico and published in 1946 under the title *El contemplado* (*The Contemplated Sea*) is his most serene. For three years, he wrote every day at a table set up for him in the open air on the terrace of the Afda Club of San Juan, facing the Caribbean Sea, his beloved *Contemplado*. He was also quite active in the island's literary and academic life, and had a hand in the founding of the literary magazine *Asomante*, published by former students of the University of Puerto Rico. After the end of the World War, he was able to travel to South America (summer of 1947) and made one trip back to Europe (excluding Spain), in 1949. This trip was a revelation, and he came back more convinced than ever that any hope for the future of civilization was still with the Old World and that the cultural axis had not shifted to America, in spite of the disaster of the second World War.

In February, 1951, Salinas had his last public triumph, with

the premiere performance of his first one-act play at New York's
Columbia University. Soon afterward, his health began to
deteriorate. Although he was still able to teach that summer
at Middlebury, his illness, eventually diagnosed as an incurable cancer, progressed rapidly in just a few months. In November, he entered Boston's Massachusetts General Hospital, and
there he died, on December 4, 1951. As requested in his will,
his body was flown to Puerto Rico and buried by the sea, in
San Juan's old Santa Magdalena Cemetery.

Everyone who met Salinas, even only casually, was impressed
by his cordiality, his ability to put people at ease, and his
eagerness to share ideas on a great variety of subjects. Most
were struck by his cosmopolitanism. Physically, he did not look
like a "typical Spaniard," since he was fair-skinned, and had
blue eyes and light hair. Lowell Dunham, who as a member
of a government cultural mission met Salinas in Puerto Rico in
1945, describes him as "a rather heavy-set man, with shoulders
that were beginning to stoop; . . . [and] more of the coloring
and appearance of a good, comfort-loving Austrian burgher
than of a hard-bitten son of Castile." The same witness was
amazed by his vast knowledge of American literary currents,
new criticism, and sociology: "I was aware that here was a
man with a vast cosmopolitan character, one of the great con-
versationalists of his days."[7] Similar statements by colleagues
and former students are also found in the memorial issues of
Hispania, Buenos Aires Literaria, Asomante, and *Insula,* published following the poet's death.

Salinas' correspondence[8] reveals a sentimental man for whom
friends and family were sacred. He particularly delighted in
the company of his two children, and later, his grandchildren.
Vicente Aleixandre relates an anecdote which stresses this deeply
human private personality. He arrived at Salinas' Madrid
residence one day, and was told that the poet was working.
As he entered the study, he saw that his friend was indeed
writing, but in an atmosphere which seemed to defy creative concentration:

I stood at the door for a few moments, astonished, and surveyed
the scene . . . the little girl was standing on her father's lap, with

both arms around his neck . . . singing strident words in his kissed
ear . . . the boy was hanging from the arm that was trying to write,
and was indeed writing. . . . A child swinging from a vine of sap
and light—the arm of a poet communicating with us.

This formless heap collapsed and Pedro Salinas stood up laughing:
"You have caught me *infraganti*." . . . He showed me the paper.
On the page, Heaven knows how, the poem had been written:
*Estoy pensando, es de noche/ en el día que hará allí,/ donde esta
noche es de día . . .*[9]

(See this poem and its translation on pp. 57–58.)

II   *The Aesthetic Principle*

In a tribute to his friend Salinas, Jorge Guillén once wrote
of him: "Seldom has any man achieved such a harmonious
balance of poet, critic, and teacher."[10] Guillén knew that for
Salinas the three activities were mutually complementing and
nearly equal in importance. His love of teaching and the
meticulous care with which he prepared each class lecture
became as legendary as it was rare in its days. Once, during one
of Guillén's visits at Johns Hopkins, Salinas remarked—only
half in jest: "They require us to teach literature, and they pay
us money besides!"[11] Most of Salinas' published literary criticism was derived directly from this teaching which his students,
both in Spain and in America, remember as always seeking to
enhance permanent values, assimilable and pertinent to each
individual's experience.[12] Salinas' essays vibrate with his personality. He is never afraid to take a reader into the confidence
of his personal feelings and opinions. At the same time, his
critical writings and scholarly editions can also display a
dazzling erudition and culture. The best example of this is
his definitive study of medieval literary tradition in the fifteenth century, entitled *Jorge Manrique, o tradición y originalidad*.[13] Shorter essays written some thirty years ago or more
(such as his pioneering study on Valle-Inclán's *esperpentos*)[14]
still surprise us by their definitive insight and power of synthesis.

In his book entitled *La poesía de Rubén Darío*, Salinas states
the guiding principle of his critical method: "It seems to me
that the most desirable end in studying a poet is to define his

Theme . . . distinguishing [it] carefully from secondary themes or sub-themes."[15] In another essay dealing with the novel as a genre, he reaffirms this need for the search for a writer's basic message: "In every novelist there is a unique intellectual and emotional vision of mankind, a particular conception of Human Nature."[16] For Salinas, then, a clarification of Theme—meaning world-vision—must precede and guide any formal and stylistic consideration.

III   *The Function of Poetry*

In his writings on the nature and function of poetry, Salinas shares the view, common in his "Generation," that the poet's first duty is "to name reality fully." But Salinas goes much further, for he also says that "All poetry . . . operates on one reality for the sake of creating another. . . . The poet absorbs reality but in absorbing it reacts against it, and, just as air is breathed out after undergoing a chemical change in the lungs, reality is also returned to the world, by a poetic operation."[17] What the poet has added is a "point of view"—in the Orteguian sense—unique to him. His creative intuition is a correlative force, establishing relationships between things which he was the first to perceive and will be the first to communicate. By making this new vision available to the reader, the poet enters the collective consciousness of a cultural tradition, to be shared with his contemporaries as well as future generations.

This is the primary justification for the poet's activity, and also, let us mention in passing, the only form of immortality to which Salinas believes he can aspire. For him, this last consideration is not a source of anguish (as it was for Unamuno), but a satisfying means of personal fulfillment: "Homer and Shakespeare, Horace and Ronsard are here by our side, alive and present to stir our sensibility. Absent only in their mortal flesh, they have accomplished the miracle to which they aspired in their poetry: to survive, to earn the gift of immortality."[18] The ultimate value of poetry lies in its forging of a common bond among men: "The poem born in solitude will be returned to all men; it will reach out to them and become a unifying force revealing affinities, coincidences, and the feeling that they all share in being human."[19]

Poetic language is best suited for this important role because of its special dimension. Salinas assigns it a privileged category, transcending ordinary daily language, and especially conceptual meaning. The poet gives words a new tension; even though he might use everyday language, the level of communication he achieves is neither conversational nor didactic. Like all Vanguardist poets, Salinas stressed the value of the metaphor by which the creative writer assumes godlike powers: "Every metaphor of real magnitude contains something close to a conception of the universe, to the cosmovision of the poet."[20] However, as we shall see later, Salinas himself did not rely heavily on metaphors except in his early works. In an essay on the poetry of Lorca, he later conceded that his generation might have put too much trust in the absolute value of the Image.[21] Rather than through complex imagery, poetic tension in Salinas is generally achieved by a subtle use of that internal rhythm, peculiar to modern free verse, which Jacques Maritain has called "the music of intuitive pulsions (*sic*)." Salinas also relies on an imaginative play on words with double meanings, seeking what he calls *le malentendu* as an element of surprise.[22]

IV *Reality and the Poet*

According to Salinas, the point of departure in searching for a writer's main theme is the determination of his basic attitude toward the circumstances which surround him. In *Reality and the Poet in Spanish Poetry*,[23] he used this approach to trace the evolution of Spanish poetry from medieval times to Romanticism. The works of six major poets show that in each case the interpenetration of external with psychic reality resulted in radically different reactions.

The attitude of the anonymous *juglar* of the *Cid* is one of basic objectivity. He brings to life historical feats and endows the epic hero with a proper balance of very human qualities and exemplary traits. The poet's realism consists in his selectivity and close attention to detail. This is the attitude which Salinas calls "Reproduction of Reality." It is a primitive attitude which in lyric poetry can only be a starting point, as we have seen. Jorge Manrique's fifteenth-century elegy to his father is a good example of what Salinas calls "Acceptance of Reality" —the medieval attitude of conformity with life's reverses, suffering, even death, sustained by the belief in ultimate heavenly reward. The Renaissance spirit, exemplified in the love poetry of Garcilaso de la Vega was to Salinas one of an "Idealization of Reality" where Nature and Man were seen as reflections of a higher Platonic order and as parts of a harmonious universal whole. The point of view of the mystics is analyzed as "Escape from an unstable and changing Reality" into a more secure inner world. Góngora represents a search for the sensual plenitude of each moment which Salinas calls "Exaltation of Reality." Finally, there is the Romantic attitude of nonconformity and estrangement which ends in "Revolt against Reality."

In interpreting Salinas' poetry, critics have frequently referred to the terminology of these essays and to Salinas' own highly personal comments in appraising each of the stated vital stands. They refer to the dual concept of Exterior vs. Inner Reality, while also noting a further opposition between *realidad,* and what Salinas calls *"Trasrrealidad"* (Transreality), a neologism to which he frequently referred. On this basis, Salinas' attitude toward reality is sometimes seen as a conflict deriving from his distrust of the material world (*realidad*) as transitory and impenetrable beyond the surface and his endless search for permanence and deeper meaning.

For Elsa Dehennin, Salinas is an Idealist engaged in a Romantic quest for the Absolute. She interprets the term *trasrrealidad* as referring to a "World of Essences" or "soul" of things.[24] Along the same lines, other critics talk of Neoplatonism (Judith Feldbaum, G. Díaz-Plaja)[25] or Mysticism—both terms seemingly implying a search for transcendental values of extraterrestrial implications. C. Feal Deibe sees Salinas' whole work in terms of the traditional conflict between body and soul.[26]

According to Dehennin, such an attitude could be motivated on the personal level by a search for immortality not unlike that of Miguel de Unamuno. The same critic concludes that Salinas' search for the Absolute eventually ends in the failure witnessed in the pessimism of his last works: "Salinas' original attitude is that of a man who suffers in his contact with daily

life, contingent and imprecise, and who instinctively turns away
from it . . . in seeking to define his most intimate inner self
and to survive in it . . . [as] both creator and actor of his existentialist dream."[27]

Julian Palley sees the Salinian theme as a dialectic between
Love and Nothingness—a constant wavering between Affirma-
tion of Life and Nihilistic Doubt. Palley stresses the second
element as dominant throughout Salinas' works, but he adds
that "the fact that he left us such consolation in his luminous
verses . . . proves that Love won in the end."[28] Palley does not
see in Salinas a flight from Reality (as did Dehennin) but a
penetration in a *trasmundo* (world-beyond) always joyful, as
witnessed even in Salinas' correspondence written in the midst
of great physical suffering, during the final days of his life.
Palley also sees Salinas as a mystic of sorts, in the oriental-
pantheistic sense.[29]

The position of both of these critics, though not entirely mistaken, seems to me exaggerated because they falsify Salinas'
personality in presenting him as a struggling *agonista*. Salinas
was, in fact, neither a rebel nor an angel. The Existential view
implies basic preoccupations with the Absurd, with Man's Fate,
and with individual immortality which are not to be found
as dominant themes in Salinas' poetry. His basic love of life
guarded him from disillusion and despair except in passing
moments of crisis and also prevented him from seeking permanent solutions in a Platonic world of the spirit.

Olga Costa Viva rightly stresses the eclectic nature of Salinas'
attitude as a fluctuating feeling which may go from doubt to
exaltation, from acceptance to idealization, from escape to
revolt. Costa Viva sees in this flexible stand the mark of Modern
Man. It is from this attitude that Man shows his dignity and
the mark of his greatness.[30]

This view, which encompasses all the positions envisioned
by Salinas, is closer to the truth, although it may give the
mistaken impression that all of these positions carry equal
weight. In subsequent chapters I shall attempt to show that
Salinas' attitude is basically one of "Acceptance of Reality" which
begins and ends with praise of life. It should be made clear
from the start that Salinas does not seek answers outside this

world, and that, as I have stated, the only immortality he believed in was the one he hoped to achieve through his works.

This is not to say that, as a man, Salinas was completely free of doubt and anguish. Critics have been right in noting that, as a result of Salinas' frustrated attempt to see beyond the illusion of shifting appearances, he became a philosophical skeptic. This is a frequent attitude, exemplified particularly in his early works. He often sought refuge in introspective contemplation, less fluid and less subject to the corrosion of time. Like Lorca he felt the need to compensate stark Reality with Dream. Certainly, Salinas' basic attitude cannot be compared with Guillén's total acceptance and even idealization of the world outside as a perfectly harmonious entity.

The only evidence of a revolt against reality occurs in Salinas' late works, when he came to perceive the modern world as a threat against man. Like Lorca and Alberti before him, he came to see urban life as depersonalizing and fostering blind conformity. He scorned the tendency to place value only on empirical facts and measures, and on pragmatic efficiency. He believed that science might ultimately kill all the individuality and therefore all new perspectives on the world. But he saw in technology an even greater threat. One of his greatest poems, "Cero" ("Zero"), and his only novel, *La bomba increíble* (*The Incredible Bomb*), are outcries against war and the possibility of total destruction. In "Zero," written in 1944, Salinas came close to predicting atomic warfare which would destroy in one instant not only the present world population, but also the collective consciousness amassed in civilization. Centuries of human experience, many generations of accrued tradition and insight in shaping human values would be lost, and only then would the word "Void" acquire real meaning. For this reason, Salinas said that the function of poetry in a mechanized world might truly be "the magnificent revolt of the poetic world against the real world."[31]

Alma de Zubizarreta has noted that most of Salinas' poetry is set in various forms of dialogue which aptly reflect his ambivalent attitude toward the world.[32] But there is really no contradiction between Salinas' love of life and his distrust of reality, or between love of Woman and fear of never possessing

her ultimate essence. Angel del Río has perhaps given us the
most accurate insight into Salinas' vital outlook. "The goal to
which the poet aspires in his contemplative vocation is immutability and silence." But since this is an impossible position in
these modern times, Salinas has chosen as an alternative "a
generous pledge to Life and to the World outside—the only
possible consolation in times lacking religious or transcendent
belief.[33]

Salinas himself said that his values corresponded to those
expressed in "Cara a Cara" ("Face to Face"), the last poem in
Guillén's *Cántico* (*Canticle*). This poem's final verses especially
sum up a whole philosophy of life, expressing solidarity with
human suffering, but also a basic belief in the beauty of everyday life, and faith in the world's future.[34]

And elsewhere, from his interpretation of Jorge Manrique's
Coplas, Salinas invites us to draw the following lesson: "Accept
reality with all its risk of being transitory and unreal, with all
its dreamlike adventure. Only he who accepts death and dreams
accepts life."[35]

CHAPTER 3

Basic Themes and Experimental Techniques in the Vanguardist Period:

(Presages, Steadfast Chance, Fable and Sign)

SALINAS' poetry can be divided into three phases of thematic and stylistic development. The first phase, his period of experimentation, includes three books of poetry, written between 1918 and 1931: *Presagios* (*Presages*), 1923, *Seguro azar* (*Steadfast Chance*), 1929, and *Fábula y signo* (*Fable and Sign*), 1931. The two books which follow, *La voz a ti debida* (*The Voice Owed to You*), 1933, and *Razón de amor* (*Love's Reason*), 1936, form a continuous cycle of love poetry, corresponding to Salinas' second phase. Many critics consider this cycle to be Salinas' best, or at any rate the most representative of his mature technique and personality. The last phase includes all the poetry written during Salinas' years of residence in the United States and Puerto Rico. Two books, *El contemplado* (*The Contemplated Sea*), 1946, and *Todo más claro* (*All Things Made Clearer*), 1949, were published during Salinas' lifetime, while *Confianza* (*Confidence*), 1954, is a posthumous collection of poems which Salinas had written some ten years previously but never quite readied for publication, although he clearly viewed them as forming one volume.[1] The last phase shows divergent moods, ranging from anguish, in parts of *All Things Made Clearer*, to optimistic praise of life in *Confidence* and near mystic exaltation in *The Contemplated Sea*. In spite of these differences, all the poetry included in these last three books reflects a new, mature outlook on life, within which all the conflicts evident up to *Love's Reason* are ultimately resolved.

I *The Poetic Function as Theme*

Salinas' first three books of verse form a unit because they represent three progressive steps in formulating his basic position, as man and as poet, toward reality, and in dealing with the related question of the proper function of poetry. *Presages* contains forty-nine poems, *Steadfast Chance* fifty, and *Fable and Sign* thirty-three. Out of a total of 132 poems, thirty-three deal directly with some aspect of the poetic process, and twenty-nine have as their theme the ambiguous nature of reality: deceitful appearance vs. the real essence of things. In addition, the same theme is implicitly contained in some twenty poems which deal either with the elusive nature of love or with the ultimate inaccessibility of the beloved. As we shall see, each book shows a conflict between a basic skepticism, which encourages Salinas to withdraw from the external world, and an irrepressible love of life which constantly brings him back to it.

The title of each volume indicates a step in the poetic process. The word "Presages" (which Salinas understood in its etymological meaning: *prae-sagire*, or "before perception")[2] is an allusion to the first affective contact with reality and a foreboding of deeper meanings behind surface appearance. *Steadfast Chance* refers to the significant moment in which the encounter of external reality with the poet's memory may result in a chance discovery or a fresh insight into reality. *Fable and Sign* distinguishes between the two aspects of reality, before and after its poetic transformation. External reality is the point of departure (or "sign") which is necessary to set the poetic process in motion. The choice of the word "Fable" in reference to the end result implies that the poet seeks to rise above an objective vision by creating new myths.

None of the three books is rigidly structured, although there are significant clusters of obviously related poems in each. The poems included in *Presages,* unlike those of the other two books, are untitled and can be referred to only by number. Most of *Presages* was written between 1920 and 1923, though there are also some earlier poems. Two sonnets for instance, Nos. 24 and 25, first appeared in the literary supplement of a Madrid daily in 1918.[3]

Presages is Salinas' most varied book as far as technique is concerned. Some poems are based on literary reminiscences from Golden Age poets. In one of the sonnets just mentioned (No. 25), there is a clear echo of both Góngora and Calderón in the last two verses of the first quatrain: *El lírico hipógrifo sueños pace,/ inclinada la testa en la pradera* (The lyrical hippogriff grazes on dreams, / with its head bent upon the meadow); while the first verse of the second tercet, *la vida al interior panal se rinde* ([all] life is stilled within the recondite labyrinth [of the soul]), was probably inspired by Fray Luis de León. Influences of Bécquer and Juan Ramón Jiménez (in Nos. 30 and 35) are also easily traceable. Save for one or two exceptions, these classical and modern sources are not as immediately apparent in later works, though, as we shall see, stylistic features inspired by the poetry of Fray Luis will later become distinctive traits of Salinian technique. Another feature present in *Presages* which will completely disappear later is the use of popular sayings, as in No. 43, *El río va a su negocio/ corre que te correrás . . .* (The river goes about its business/ flowing as it will . . .), or of a colloquial and sometimes flippant style reminiscent of Antonio Machado's *Proverbios y cantares* (Nos. 29 and 33).

The first five poems of *Presages,* including a five-verse introductory epigraph, can be seen as forming a kind of initial aesthetic creed. The five introductory verses underline the poet's awareness of his temporal and spatial circumstances, seen not as limitations, but as forming the necessary concrete starting point of all poetry:

Forjé un eslabón un día
otro día forjé otro
y otro.
De pronto se me juntaron
—era la cadena—todos. (p. 51)[4]

(I fashioned a chainlink one day
On the next day I forged another
and another.
Soon I found them all joined together
and between them they formed the chain.)

The chain of life is made up of each momentary contact with
the material world, and poetry, ideally, joins these moments in
a creative whole. Tangible reality as perceived in each moment
is thus the necessary poetic raw material, as the following poem
(No. 1) explicitly states:

> *Suelo. Nada más.*
> *Suelo. Nada menos.*
> *Y que te baste con eso.*
> *Porque en el suelo los pies hincados,*
> *en los pies torso derecho,*
> *en el torso la testa firme,*
> *y allá, al socaire de la frente,*
> *la idea pura, y en la idea pura*
> *el mañana, la llave*
> *—mañana—de lo eterno.* (p. 53)

> (Ground. Nothing more.
> Ground. Nothing less.
> And with that be content.
> For on the ground the feet are thrust,
> Upon the feet, the body erect,
> and on the body, firmly, the head;
> and there, within the confines of the brow,
> pure idea, and within pure idea
> tomorrow's promise—the key
> —tomorrow—of the eternal.)

The reference to "pure idea" and to a realm of "eternal"
absolutes is cited by some critics as evidence of Salinas' neoplatonic tendencies. To me, it is merely indicative of a search,
the exact nature of which Salinas does not clarify at this point.
He is aware that poetry, beginning with concrete reality, must
end elsewhere, but he has not yet perceived the true nature of
what he will later call *trasrrealidad*. For the moment, the poetic
adventure toward the Absolute is stated only in a rather conventional Idealist stand.

Poems 2 and 3 pursue the meditation on the nature of Poetry.
No. 2 is a warning about what poetry should not try to do: deal
in abstract speculations. The poem, set in the form of a dialogue
with a swiftly flowing stream, expresses the timeless metaphysical

problem concerning what forms the essential, as opposed to the accidental aspects of a thing:

> *Agua de la noche, serpiente indecisa,*
> *silbo menor y rumbo ignorado;*
> *¿qué día nieve, qué día mar? Dime.*
> . . . .
> *—No te lo diré: entre tus labios me tienes,*
> *beso te doy pero no claridades.*
> . . . .
> *[. . . . .]⁵ porque yo he sido hecha*
> *para la sed de los labios que nunca preguntan.* (p. 54)

> (Water in the night, [thou] indecisive serpent
> with a hushed hiss, and course unknown;
> snow? On what day? Sea? On what day? Tell me.
> . . . .
> I shall not tell you; you have me on your lips,
> I give you kisses, but I do not enlighten.
> . . . .
> . . . . for I was made
> for the thirst of lips that never ask.)

Poetic intuition which may result in a direct insight into reality at any given moment: *beso te doy* cannot easily translate that particular moment. The dilemma of poetic expression lies in the attempt to preserve in timeless form an experience which is perceived in the flux of existence. It is the dilemma which Antonio Machado has also expressed in a well-known poem (No. XXXV from *Proverbios y Cantares*), which I shall translate here in part, by way of analogy. Machado talks about two ways of knowing, one obviously referring to Bergsonian intuition, the other to rational knowledge, also an imperfect instrument where poetry is concerned. And so, he asks ironically:

> Tell me, [therefore]: which is better?
> a visionary consciousness
> gazing into the deep aquarium
> at live
> fugitive fish,
> which cannot be fished out,

or the accursed task
of forever throwing on the sand
the dead fish from the sea?[6]

The dilemma which poetry strives to resolve is that of preserving
and communicating an experience without abstracting from
any of its paradoxical complexities. Both Machado and Salinas
throughout their works searched in vain for a wholly satisfactory
solution to this problem.

Returning to *Presages*, we encounter in No. 3 another analogy.
The poet's "blindman's hand" will not seize a tempting fruit
from a tree branch because: ... *tiene/ ambiciones más profun-
das/ que la de los ojos/ ... eterna ambición de asir/ lo inasidero*
(... it has/ ambitions deeper than that of the eyes/ ... eternal
ambition of reaching/ for the unreachable). Faced with this
impossible task, the temptation (in this poem, and repeatedly
throughout the book) will be to seek isolation in an introspective
world where reality is not constantly changing and where
objects exist only as foils for the projection of personal feelings.
In this inner world, the creator's hands are at rest: *asidas ansia
con ansia/ y deseo con deseo* (clasped together as eagerness
with eagerness/ and desire with desire). This however, is only
a momentary temptation. The last verses of the poem are Salinas'
self-urge to continue his search: *Mano de ciego no es ciega:/
una voluntad la manda,/ no los ojos de su dueño* ([The] blindman's hand is not blind:/ a will guides it,/ not the eyes of
its owner).

In the final poem of this series an implied comparison is made
between the poet and his infant daughter who greets every new
sensation with exuberant enthusiasm, but can express her feelings
with only two incomprehensible words: Tatá, Dadá, so that she
is unable to communicate anything more precise than her spontaneous joy:

"Todo lo confunde," dijo	("She confuses everything," said
su madre. Y era verdad	her mother. And it was true.
Porque cuando yo la oía	Because as I heard her
decir "Tatá, Dadá,"	say "Tata, Dada,"
veía la bola del mundo	I could see the ball of the world
rodar, rodar,	roll and roll,

· ·

el mar, las montañas, todo	the sea, the mountains, everything
hecho una bola confusa;	tumbling together in a ball;
el mundo "Tatá, Dadá." (p. 56)	the world, a "Tata, Dada.")*

The five opening poems of *Presages* thus complete each other and summarize the general feelings expressed in the book. Its characteristic trait, says Angel del Río, is the position of the poet always situating himself on the edge between reality and inner life... because all the material world seems to him an illusion, despite its exact appearance.[7]

If a single poem could be chosen to illustrate Salinas' attitude toward reality at this time, it might be No. 20:

Estos dulces vocablos con que me estás hablando
no los entiendo, paisaje,
no son los míos.
Te diriges a mí con arboledas
suavísimas, con una ría mansa y clara
y con trinos de ave.
Y yo aprendí otra cosa: la encina dura y seca
en una tierra pobre, sin agua, y a lo lejos,
come dechado, el águila,
y como negra realidad, el negro cuervo.
Pero es tan dulce el son de ese tu no aprendido
lenguaje, que presiente el alma en él la escala
por donde bajarán los secretos divinos.
Y ansioso y torpe, a tu vera me quedo
esperando que tú me enseñes el lenguaje
que no es mío, con unas incógnitas palabras
sin sentido.
Y que me lleves a la claridad de lo incognoscible,
paisaje dulce, por vocablos desconocidos. (p. 74)

(I do not understand, oh countryside,
the soft words with which you speak to me;
they are not mine.
You speak to me with gentle groves,
with a tame and clear stream
and with the trills of birds.
I had learned other things: the hard, dry oak
in a bleak land, without water, in the distance,

the eagle as a model,
and as somber reality, the black crow.
Yet, so sweet is the sound of your unlearned
language, that the soul presages in it a ladder
down which divine secrets will be descending.
And eager but clumsy, I remain by your side
waiting for you to teach me the language
that is not mine, with unknown
meaningless words.
And for you to lead me toward the clarity of the unknowable,
sweet countryside, with unknown words.)

The poem, like so many others in *Presages*, is inspired by
Nature, in this case the contemplation of a landscape different
from Salinas' native Castile. The poet is deeply moved by its
beauty but unable to understand his experience fully and to
translate it into words. The unknown language with which
Nature "speaks" to him succeeds only in evoking a "presenti-
ment" or new visions, as yet mysterious to him, but which he
does not despair of discovering.

II   *The Concrete World as Illusion*

While writing *Presages*, Salinas was also at work on a series
of prose sketches published under the title *Víspera del gozo*
(*On the Eve of Joy*), in 1926. These sketches are not really
stories, since they lack a conventional narrative structure. Each
anecdote, says Angel del Río, is but a pretext to express the
interior excitement of the imminent joy of possession—of woman,
city, or landscape—a joy which is soon shattered, and never
achieved.[8] In No. 5 of *Presages*, Salinas had expressed this feeling in the final verse of the poem: *Felicidad, alma sin cuerpo,/
sombra pura* ... (Happiness, thou soulless body, thou pure
shadow).

There are nine love poems in *Presages*. Three of them (Nos.
18, 35, and 41) show the value which Salinas placed on love
as the best means of communication, capable of giving lovers
a higher collective identity. This exaltation of love will later be
the central theme in *The Voice Owed to You*. But five of *Presages'* love poems (8, 14, 34, 36, and 37) have to do with the

ephemeral nature of love and the endless search for the beloved's real identity.

Number 8 is one of the best poems of *Presages* and one which already exemplifies Salinas' later technique of beginning a poem not at the point of his direct perception of reality, but as a meditation through which it is already being recreated in a series of analogies and paradoxes:

*¡Cuánto rato te he mirado
sin mirarte a ti, en la imagen
exacta e inaccesible
que te traiciona el espejo!
"Bésame," dices. Te beso,
y mientras te beso pienso
en lo fríos que serán
tus labios en el espejo.
"Toda el alma para ti,"*

murmuras, pero en el pecho

*siento un vacío que sólo
me lo llenará ese alma
que no me das.
El alma que se recata
con disfraz de claridades
en tu forma del espejo.* (p. 60)

(So often, I have looked at you
not seeing you, but the image
exact and inaccessible
offered by the mirror's deception!
"Kiss me," you say. I kiss you:
and kissing you, I think of
how very cold your lips might be
in [the reflection of] the mirror.
You whisper softly: "My soul's
yours"
but [meanwhile], I, within my
breast
feel an emptiness that [I know]
could only be filled by that soul
which you won't give me.
The soul which, concealing itself
with clarity as its disguise,
is taking your shape in the mirror.)

Thus, we see that to express the impossibility of ever possessing the woman's real self, Salinas compares her concrete presence in the form of words and kisses to a mirage as intangible as a mirror reflection. The last three verses, especially, show the poet's frustration as he sees reality—the real essence or soul of Being—deliberately flaunting him in the form of ever deceitful illusions of forms and shapes.

The last poem in the book (No. 49) carries the poet one step further as a logical consequence of his distrustful attitude toward love. To the concrete presence of the beloved, now within his reach, he prefers the image which he will recreate in his imagination, and which, embellished with memories and transformed by dreams, he will be able to recall at will, years

later, when the two lovers will remember each other only in
vague and distant memories, or might even be separated by
death:

Te llamaré mañana,	(I'll call you tomorrow,
. . . .	. . . .
[. . . . .] cuando estés	. . . . when you might be
allá detrás de una	somewhere far behind a
frágil pared de vientos,	fragile barrier of winds,
de cielos y de años. (p. 103)	of skies and of years.)

This attitude is equivalent to the introspective dream which
we have already seen expressed in connection with the previous
theme. It is a temporary wish to escape from reality, brought
about by an overwhelming desire for *quietud* and for a more
rigorous and secure world than that which presents itself to
his eyes.[9]

III *The Dynamic Pace of Modern Life*

Steadfast Chance marks Salinas' full adherence to the spirit
of Ultraism as it was first assimilated by the Generation of 1927.
In fact, both in spirit and in style, the book (written between
1924 and 1928) could well be chosen as a prototype of the
group's initial period.

The predominant attitude is now one of marvelling discovery
of the everyday world. The mood is generally optimistic, and
several poems recall, both in tone and technique, the exuberant
praise of life of Guillén's *Cántico* (e.g., No. 18). Salinas seeks to
show harmony and almost geometric perfection in each appre-
hended moment. As in Cubistic painting, objects are often
reduced to their essential lines, and Salinas strives for a concise,
almost telegraphic, style by eliminating connecting words such
as articles and conjunctions. Verbs are used very sparingly,
especially those which suggest movement. To further underline
this static quality, Salinas prefers to use an infinitive or gerund
where one would normally expect a conjugated verb. We find
examples of this in No. 19: *En el paisaje tierno/—aquí, quedarse
—/el puente de hierro* (In the soft landscape/—here, to stay—/
the iron bridge), and in No. 33, a love poem: *Tú aquí, delante.
Mirándote/ yo ¡Qué bodas/ tuyas, mías, con lo exacto!* (You

here, before me. And looking at you/ I. What marriage,/ yours, mine, with exactness!) Finally, Salinas makes frequent use of very concentrated metaphors, based either on remote visual approximations, or, more often, on mental play on words in the *conceptista* tradition. In No. 8, we find the following: *compás de los horizontes/ el pico de las cigüenas* (Compass [i.e., for drawing] of the horizons/ the beaks of the storks). A few poems, as No. 17, offer a succession of defining images which, like Gómez de la Serna's *greguerías,* emphasize rapidly changing sensations:

El mar. Chasquido breve,	(The sea. A whip cracks briefly
muerte de adolescencia	the death of adolescence
sobre la arena tibia.	on the lukewarm sand.
Playa.	A beach.
. . . .	. . . .
El mar. Embate plano	The sea. Horizontal charge
contra rocas tajadas.	against the steep-faced rock.
Escribe blanca espuma	The white foam is writing
en el cantil su acróstico.	its acrostic upon the cliff.
Se lo descifra el viento.	The wind deciphers it.
Secreto. (p. 123)	A secret.)*

Many poems of *Steadfast Chance* are inspired by those modern inventions which have revolutionized man's perception of time and distance, and have created a new life-rhythm. In No. 10, "Navacerrada, abril" ("Navacerrada, April"), the first of Salinas' Futuristic poems, the automobile becomes a partner to the poet's discovery:

Los dos solos. ¡Qué bien	(The two of us, alone. How happy
aquí, en el puerto, altos!	here, up high, in the mountain pass!
Vencido verde, triunfo	A green conquest, a triumph
de los dos, al venir	of us both, as we pass
queda un paisaje atrás:	a landscape left behind:
otro enfrente, esperándonos.	another before us, awaiting.
. . . .	. . . .
Alma mía en la tuya	My soul embraces your
mecánica; mi fuerza	mechanical soul, my strength
bien medida la tuya	well gauged and yours
justa: doce caballos. (p. 116)	exact: twelve horsepower.)

In No. 27, "35 Bujías" ("35 Kilowatts"), Salinas praises an electric lightbulb for much the same reason:

> descifraremos formas leves, signos,
> perseguidos en mares de blancura
> por mí, por ella, artificial princesa,
> amada eléctrica. (p. 136)

> (We shall decipher vague shapes and signs
> pursued in oceans of whiteness
> by me, by her, the artificial princess,
> electric lover.)

The cinema is a source of new myths, as in No. 26, "Cinematógrafo" ("Cinematograph"), but it also becomes a new adequate symbol of the deceitfulness of appearances. "Far West," (sic) No. 15, begins with a baroque image, wonderfully suggestive of impetuous movement and probably inspired by the beginning verses of Calderón's *Life Is a Dream*:

> ¡Qué viento a ocho mil kilómetros!
> . . . .
> ¿No ves los cabellos sueltos
> de Mabel, la caballista
> que entorna los ojos limpios
> ella, viento, contra el viento?

> (What a wind at eight thousand kilometers per hour!
> . . . .
> Don't you see the loose hair
> of Mabel, the horsewoman
> closing her limpid eyes:
> Wind herself against the wind?)

But all this burst of activity which takes place only intangibly on a screen has a dreamlike quality. It fascinates the poet but also frustrates him:

> Sí le veo, sin sentirle.   (I see it, yes, but I don't feel it.
> Está allí, en el mundo suyo,   It remains there in its own world;
> viento de cine, ese viento. (p. 121)   that wind [is] a pictorial wind.)

"Far West" is one of the poems which prove that beneath Salinas' new enthusiasm for modern artifacts he has not abandoned earlier preoccupations. Nine poems of *Steadfast Chance* deal with the equivocal nature of reality, and twelve love poems also repeat previous attitudes. Such conflicting stands show only that when Salinas gives in to spontaneous reactions, his irrepressible love of life, in all its excitement and variety, can temporarily overcome a skepticism which is born of reflection. But sooner or later, Salinas always returns to his search for a deeper and more lasting reality and to his defense of poetry's role in revealing *la trasrrealidad.*

IV   Concrete Reality Transformed by the Imagination

The poems of *Steadfast Chance* which deal with Salinas' aesthetics no longer center, as did those in *Presages*, around the initial impact of an object's discovery, but rather on the process of its transformation by means of intuitive associations.

No. 4, "Vocación" ("Vocation"), is particularly significant in establishing the limits and differences between outer and inner worlds, and in making a first allusion to the nature of this "trans-reality":

Abrir los ojos. Y ver
sin falta ni sobra, a colmo

en la luz clara del día,
perfecto el mundo, completo.
. . . .
Todo en el fiel. Pero yo . . .
Tú, de sobra. A mirar,
y nada más que a mirar
la belleza rematada

que ya no te necesita.
Cerrar los ojos. Y ver
incompleto, tembloroso,
de será o de no será,
—masas torpes, planos sordos—
sin luz, sin gracia, sin orden

(To open my eyes. And to see
Neither needing nor exceeding,
    but abundant
in the clarity of daylight,
a perfect, a complete world.
. . . .
Everything in balance, but I . . .
but you, superfluous. Looking on,
and only looking on, upon
the thoroughly accomplished
    beauty
which is no longer in need of you.
To close my eyes. And to see
incomplete and trembling,
not knowing if it will take form
—clumsy masses, dull surfaces—
without light, without grace or
    order

un mundo sin acabar,	an unfinished world,
necesitado, llamándome	in need of me and calling me.
a mí, o a ti o a cualquiera	Me, or you, or anyone
que ponga lo que le falta,	who might give it what it lacks,
que le dé la perfección.	who might give it its perfection.
En aquella tarde clara,	And on that sunny afternoon
en aquel mundo sin tacha,	in that untarnished innocent world
escogí:	I chose:
el otro.	the other.
Cerré los ojos. (p. 110)	I closed my eyes.) *

The poem, consistant with the mood of *Steadfast Chance*, begins with a declaration of faith in life, evident in the first four verses. Yet it ends on what appears to be a withdrawal into a private unreal world. In spite of this ending, the poem does not indicate an attempt to escape from reality (as some critics have suggested). Rather, it is a temporary retreat during which reality as perceived will be enriched with the wisdom of a new "point of view," the "I" implied in Ortega y Gasset's remark: "I am I and my circumstances." It is to be noted that Salinas, in his function of interpreter of reality, does not assign to himself the privileged position of a Romantic seer. The addition of any new point of view, *a mí, a ti, o a cualquiera* . . . , will always enrich the collective consciousness. Salinas was most certainly influenced by Ortega's "perspectivism" in his idea of the mission of culture, and of art in particular, in preserving and constantly adding new perspectives with which to appraise reality.

The nature of a constant interchange between outer and inner worlds is thus ultimately defined in *Steadfast Chance*. The poet interprets reality and re-creates it in a poem. But the poem will do more than just communicate a certain world-vision through a special perspective; it will also create a new myth, which will render life as less conventionally precise, richer in imaginative overtones, and therefore more acceptable in the face of disillusion. This is the implied message contained in Salinas' third book of verse, *Fable and Sign*.

In this book, Salinas does not introduce any theme or technique not already present in his earlier poetry. The fascination with technical progress and big-city life is still evident —though to a lesser degree—in poems such as "Underwood Girls," No. 28, in praise of the typewriter as "partner" in the act of creation, or in the evocation of a permanent ideal Spring in a Paris shop window, in No. 7: "Paris, abril, modelo" ("Paris, April, Model"). In No. 9, "Amsterdam," the city is described solely in terms of neon signs flashing in the night: *verdes, rojos, azules, rapidísimas/ luces extrañas por los ojos/ [...] anuncios luminosos de la vida* (green, red, blue, swiftest/ lights dazzling to the eye/ ... luminous signs of life). These city lights are, for the moment, still regarded as elements of beauty and throbbing excitement. As we shall see later, they will be evoked in *All Things Made Clearer* to symbolize a civilization tied to artificial and dehumanizing values.

Already in *Fable and Sign* there is a noticeable change in the poet's appraisal of the material world. The prevailing mood is no longer one of carefree enjoyment of the here and now. Salinas still praises life, but he does so rather stoically, with the full realization that all human and material existence is engaged in a frenetic race with death. Repeatedly, Salinas evokes man's vain wish to abolish the destructive force of time, as in No. 2, "Reló pintado" ("Painted Clock"), and to delay the fatal plunge into the void. J. Palley's observation on Salinas' obsession with Nothingness holds true in this book. Even E. Dehennin, when confronted with the initial poem, "La orilla" ("The Brink") concedes that "for once ... despair leads Salinas to disavow his quest for the Absolute."[10] Yet, Salinas' ultimate stand is not one of despair but, rather, qualified resignation and conformity with man's fate. The poem is set in the form of a monologue (the *tú* here refers to the speaker himself):

Basta, no hay que pedir más,	(It's enough, do not ask for more,
luz, amor, treinta de abril.	light, love, thirtieth of April.
Hay que fingir que ya tienes	Pretend that you already have
bastante, que estás saciado,	enough; that you are satisfied,
que te sobra lo que queda	and that you cannot use what's left
de abril	of April
después del treinta de abril.	after this thirtieth of April.

Dejarlo,	Forget it,
como si pudiera darte	as if April could give you
más y tú no lo quisieras.	more, and you'd refuse.
Porque así te irás creído	In doing so you'll leave content
que no se acababa nunca	not seeing [there], already dying,
lo que estaba muriendo.	what you believed would never end.
Te irás	You'll leave
sin sospechar que estuviste	without suspecting that you'd reached
allí al borde de lo último.	the brink of all finality.
Porque aquello, fecha, beso	Because all things, the date, the kiss
—cuando tú te despediste	—when [at last] you bid your farewell
te parecía lo eterno—,	believing them to be eternal—
era lo último.	were at an end.
Detrás	Beyond,
el fin sin remedio, el fondo	the true finality, the hard
duro y seco de la nada.	and dry abyss of the void.
Lo que hubieses visto tú,	What you yourself might well have seen
si llegas a pedir más	if you had dared to ask for more
abril al treinta de abril. (p. 165)	April from the thirtieth of April.)

Throughout *Fable and Sign*, the least permanent elements are material objects, and their only hope for survival is the succession of viewers capable of endowing them with a new life, a new soul. This can best be illustrated in the comparison of three poems inspired by the contemplation of the architectural mass of *San Lorenzo del Escorial*, the palace-monastery built by Philip II in 1563. With its perfectly geometric proportions, the palace is a perfect symbol of permanence and solidity, and a monument to man's defiance of time. It is this concept that Salinas evokes in "Escorial II," No. 24, where he ironically attempts to abstract the very essence of the building and its surrounding landscape in terms of its sheer numerical proportions. They are so perfect that they should leave no room for doubt, or for fantasy:

En vez de soñar, contar.	(Instead of dreaming, count.
La fachada del oeste	Six hundred twelve windows abreast

tiene	are in
seiscientas doce ventanas.	the line that faces West.
. . . .	. . . .
Y ya no podrá escapárseme	The morning cannot flee me
en las volandas del sueño	in her dream-wings clad.
la mañana. Haré la raya	Now I shall draw the line
para ir sumando: seiscientas	and add: six hundred
doce, más cinco, más tres,	twelve, plus five, plus three
más doce.	plus twelve.
¡Qué felicidad igual	What joy is equal to
a seiscientos treinta y dos!	six hundred and thirty-two!
En abril, al mediodía,	An April noon, and here,
cuenta clara. (p. 196)	the reckoning clear.)[11]

The conclusion is sadly ironic; one cannot take seriously, when dealing with Salinas, values based solely on mathematical proof, to the exclusion of dream. The poem only emphasizes the paradox implied in the building's perfection. *El Escorial* was built as a monument to Christian faith and as a symbol of Philip's quest for Catholic supremacy. The message is outdated. It is the death of an ideal that is now evoked, eternally frozen in granite. This is the meaning implied in the verses from "Escorial I" (No. 20):

De estar tan hecho	(It is so utterly finished
ya se le acabó el querer.	that it has lost the desire to want.
Lo que quiso es ahora piedra,	What once it wanted is now stone,
dimensión, forma. Y da miedo	dimension, form. It chills
de que esté ya más arriba	[to see] that now it has reached
del vivir, al otro lado. (p. 191)	the other side of life.)*

Finally, in "Jardín de los Frailes" ("The Friars' Garden"), No. 22, we witness the creation of the "fable." The building is reborn in a subtle movement of lines, swayed by the summer breeze in the garden's reflecting pool, against a soft background of sky and vegetation:

Se te quebraron las rectas,	(Your straight lines thrust away their bonds,
los planos se te arqueaban	your planes curved themselves into arcs

para vivir, como el pecho.	to feel life, as a [human] breast.
¡Qué latido	How your heart beat,
en ansias verdes, azules,	[trembling] with green and blue desires,
en ondas, contra los siglos	in the clear waters, against unbending
rectilíneos!	centuries!
. . . .	. . . .
Tu alma, tan insospechada,	Your soul, that no one knew existed,
suelta ya de su cadáver	freed at last from a frigid corpse,
que seguía allí lo mismo	that yet remained, immutable
—monumento nacional—,	—[as a] national monument—,
en su sitio, para siempre.	still in its place, and there forever.
El agua te sacó el alma.[12] (p. 193)	The water brought out your soul.)

This new lease on life is of course a product of the poet's imagination, but for anyone contemplating the building, the evocation of this fable, with its subtly musical verses, will indeed add a new dimension and a dynamic quality to the somber austerity of the Guadarrama landscape.

V *Love as Illusion*

The theme of love is of greater importance than ever before in *Fable and Sign.* Of the various attitudes already discussed in connection with *Presages,* skepticism and disillusionment now prevail. Only three of the book's twelve poems on this theme can be said to show love as a fulfilling and satisfactory experience. More abundant are poems which deal with separation or estrangement, as does No. 11, "Muertes" ("Deaths"). "Ruptura sin palabras" ("A Wordless Breaking-off"), No. 21, is one of Salinas' most poignant poems about a moment of total incomprehension very close to hate. The poem begins with the description of a landscape which seems to embody the antagonism of the two lovers:

Aspero, el camino	(Pitted and rough the road
entre cerros pardos.	between brown somber hills.
Rastreros los vientos	Winds trailing in the air,
arrancaban altos	as they drew out the still

quejidos de polvo	protesting wails of dust
a la tierra triste.	from the sorrowful earth.
. . . .	. . . .
Tu mirada caía	Glances, like a blank mass
con su cuerpo blanco	fell steadily from your eyes,
siempre sobre púas,	landing on [mountain] peaks,
chumberas, picachos,	on prickly shrubs and crests,
de agrio paisaje	bristling
erizado.	in the bitter landscape.
. . . .	. . . .
En los labios secos	And meeting our parched lips
los adios expósitos	orphaned hatreds of the air,
del aire, esperando,	[quiet] as they lay in wait
sacaban el filo	sharpening wicked blades
malo al sí y al no.	of yesses and of nos.)

The poem's ending is a nostalgic lament for a happiness already irrevocably passing. One hateful moment forewarns of a future separation and of the inevitable dissolution of all human experiences and memory in time:

Sin hablar, sin nada	(Nothing, not a word spoken
sentí que ya estábamos	Yet, I felt that we stood
frente a frente. Toda	will against will. I saw you
desnuda te ví	bared [of all pretenses]
en tu yo más malo.	in your most wicked self.
Lo que yo te quise	What once I loved in you
—¡qué tiempo lentísimo!—	—in time that seemed unending—
en minutos rápidos	in rapidly ticking seconds
se iba desamando. (pp. 191-92)	was casting its love away.)*

One of my favorite poems of *Fable and Sign* is No. 31, "Luz de la noche" ("Light of Night"), another love poem dealing with the idea of separation. Its point of departure, as is often the case in Salinas, is not a direct experience, but a circumvoluted meditation expressed through an extended metaphor:

Estoy pensando, es de noche,	(I am thinking, it is nighttime,
en el día que hará allí	of the day it must be over there
donde esta noche es de día.	where this nighttime is called daytime.
En las sombrillas alegres,	Of those little cheerful shadows

abiertas todas las flores,	of all the flowers [radiantly] open
contra ese sol, que es la luna	against that sun which is this moon
tenue que me alumbra a mí.	beaming its tenuous light upon me.)

On the literal level, these verses describe life as it goes on in two different time zones. It is nighttime and life has stopped where the poet is standing, but the moonlight is the reflection of a bright, happy sun which gives warmth and joy on the other side of the earth, in a life-activity from which he feels sadly cut off.

The first part of the poem, however, is only an elaborate preparation; its whole impact comes from the reader's surprise in realizing that what the poet is describing is not joyful life in a distant land, but a woman's happy dreams, betrayed by her smile (the poet's moon) as she lies asleep beside her lover. This smile is an indication of a happy, very private world in which the poet will never be able to participate:

[. . .] pienso en el otro lado	(. . . I am thinking of the other side
de tu sueño, donde hay luz	of your sleep, where there's a light
que yo no veo.	that I do not see.
. . . .	. . . .
con esa sonrisa abierta,	with your trusting and smiling face,
tan alegre, tan de flores	so happy, like [a field of] flowers
que la noche y yo sentimos	that the night and I understand
que no puede ser de aquí.	that it could never be from here.)
(pp. 210-11)	

Stylistically, this poem is already on the threshold of Salinas' mature technique which I shall discuss in connection with *The Voice Owed to You.* Here I shall only point out the most striking use of paradox and play on words, even in the title of the poem. This preference for what Salinas called *le malentendu* is not a gratuitous baroque trait on his part. It is his way of conveying his distrust of appearances. He is constantly reminding us that we should never take surface illusions at face value; behind them, always, there is a deeper reality to be discovered.

CHAPTER 4

Love: *A Paradise Lost and Regained*
(The Voice Owed to You, Love's Reason)

I   *The Resurgence of the Love Theme in the Generation of 1927*

WHEN, in 1933, Salinas published *The Voice Owed to You,* the poetry of the Generation of 1927 had already undergone the noticeable change of mood which marked the beginning of its second period. As the carefree optimism of the 1920's ended abruptly, around the beginning of the new decade, it was followed for many by emotional crisis and a feeling of alienation in a now hostile modern world. The attitude of some of the best-known members of the group became akin to what Salinas would later describe as the Romantic revolt against reality.

Apart from this general attitude, a more definite factor which has enabled critics to refer to the Generation of 1927's second period as a neo-Romantic revival was the strong resurgence of the theme of Love viewed as the unattainable ideal, or ultimately as man's supreme illusion. For poets such as Cernuda and Alberti, the betrayal implied in the loss of this love ideal became a broad symbol for the frustrated human condition. Love was evoked in the image of a lost paradise, or as a happiness that never really existed except as a dream. Alberti's famous poem "Tres recuerdos del cielo" ("Three Remembrances of Heaven")[1]—significantly inspired by, and dedicated to, the great Romantic poet Gustavo Adolfo Bécquer —develops this theme to despairing conclusions. Aleixandre's poetry in *Espadas como labios* (*Swords like Lips*), 1932, and *La destrucción o el amor* (*Destruction Equals Love*), 1934, presents love as a clashing and frustrated encounter. It adds the concept, also Romantic in origin, of sexual passion as a

59

terrifying force underlying the perpetual cosmic cycle of creation and destruction.

At first glance, there would seem to be little similarity between the luminous verses of Salinas' great love cycle and the agitated near-Surrealistic imagery used by Alberti, Cernuda, or Aleixandre in the same period. Yet, though the means of expression were different, Salinas echoed similar conflicts, received the same Romantic influences, and made use of parallel allusions to love as biblical paradise or cosmic force. Salinas differed, however, in that he saw love not merely as an illusion or dream wished for, but as an idyllic reality whose fragility and ultimate loss was due only to its temporal limitations.

The main conflict in Salinas' love poetry arises in attempting to transcend these limitations. The problem is stated in Part One of the cycle, *The Voice Owed to You,* which describes a private love paradise, first discovered then lost. In the course of Part Two, *Love's Reason,* Salinas resolves the conflicts caused by the loss of this particular love to his satisfaction. Love for him becomes an eternal cyclic force, which, if properly understood and accepted, should give sufficient justification to all human existence. On the basis of this rediscovery of love, Salinas holds the promise of a new paradise, forever recaptured.

II *Some Structural and Thematic Paradoxes in* The Voice Owed to You *and* Love's Reason

Though most critics agree that the poetry collected in these two books is probably Salinas' best, or at any rate his first truly mature verses, they hold basically divergent views concerning both the structure and meaning of the cycle. Questions arise about whether to consider the two books as one continuous poem, as two poems, or merely as a series of variations connected only by their common love theme. *The Voice Owed to You* bears the generic subtitle of *poema,* which suggests some structural unity. Yet, the first edition divided the 2462 verses into seventy clearly independent segments or "poems," each beginning on a fresh page, with no overlapping permitted. It is soon apparent that each section was conceived and must be read on two levels, both as an entity complete in itself and as a part of the entire poem.[2] Similarly, *Love's Reason* is subtitled *poesía*, but is divided into two parts. The first 1930 verses are separated into forty-two segments, following the method of the preceding book, while eight titled poems—a total of 839 verses—make up Part II.

Faced with this paradox, most critics have chosen to minimize the importance of the subtitles and to see the book as collections of "variations" or "meditations" on the theme of love. Stephen Gilman suggests that formal ambiguity—poem or poems, whole or parts—was perhaps intentional, at least in the case of *The Voice Owed to You*. The same critic briefly considers, and rejects as overly Romantic, the possibility of a unity based on a narrative sequel: the story of a single love from beginning to end.[3] Joaquín González Muela was the first to point out that there is at least some validity to this interpretation, since the text of *The Voice Owed to You* begins with verbs in the present and future tenses—corresponding to an incipient love affair—whereas from a point which he indicates as verse 986, a progressive separation of the two lovers is evidenced in the use of past tenses.[4]

In general, critics have been puzzled by this long love poem, which, as its title indicates, seems to be addressed to a real woman, though she remains unnamed, and who is described only in the vaguest terms. As her feelings are never expressed, and the entire love experience is seen solely through its effects on the poet-protagonist, she seems almost totally absent. Thus, although in both books the beloved is addressed as *Tú*, the poem might give the impression of being more a self-searching monologue than a true dialogue.

Such is the ultimate opinion of an important group of mostly early critics. They conclude that the poem has no biographical basis and that, possibly, it does not even really deal with love. Leo Spitzer ends a lengthy and often-quoted article by saying that the poem is really "the lament of a soul who, lacking faith in God, seeks fulfillment in self-knowledge." The same critic adds: "I am acquainted with no love poetry in which the two lovers are so completely reduced to the poet's own ego. . . . This poet is really a Narcissus who knows no one outside himself."[5]

62   PEDRO   SALINAS

For Pierre Darmangeat, the beloved *Tú* is a totally imaginary being, a mere symbolic incarnation of the general concept of love.[6] G. Díaz-Plaja talks about a love affair reduced to a bare outline, without place or time, and a woman who is the projection of a Neoplatonic ideal.[7] More recently, C. B. Morris still viewed the poem as pure mental speculation, and although he does not deny the existence of a real woman, he minimizes her importance: "... to possess his *amada* would thwart Salinas' ambition to live perpetually cocooned within a love from which he excluded the banal data of time, place, and circumstances.... Salinas was more interested in probing and weighing [love]'s effects on his sensibility than in imagining what it could look like."[8] It is, of course, statements such as these which have gained Salinas a controversial reputation as an unfeeling and cerebral poet.

The opinion of the opposing group of critics[9] can best be summed up in the following statement by Jorge Guillén. "Salinas' love poetry does not give us a strange, eccentric love, but one which is perfectly normal, a love story which is fulfilled in a normal way. The story itself amounts to no more than a series of situations involving sentiment, situations which never degenerate in sentimentalism, although they retain their warmth."[10]

Such divergences concerning the basic meaning and composition of a poet suggest that there may be more than one level of interpretation intended. Salinas first published an important fragment of *The Voice Owed to You* under another title: *Amor en vilo (Love Unbound)*.[11] The same year, he adopted the more personal title, borrowed from a verse from the sixteenth-century poet Garcilaso de la Vega, for the definitive edition. The difference between the two titles points to the dual nature of the book. On one level it is a volume of sentimental memoirs from which Salinas has discreetly eliminated all personal allusions (except for two references to the young woman's age: twenty). Discretion is one reason, but a more compelling one is the wish to make the poem transcend his individual experience as a general statement on the paradoxical nature of love. This is indicated in Salinas' choice as his book's epigraph, of a verse from Shelley's *Epipsychidion*: "Thou Wonder, and Thou Beauty, and Thou Terror." As I have already mentioned, the poem is also developed on a symbolic level, based on the story of Genesis; and on the Christian concept of man's fall and salvation.

A final mention of the literary tradition which inspired the poem's form and some of its ideas will help clarify structural ambiguities. S. Gilman has shown that in the initial poem or "proem" of *The Voice Owed to You* there is a "calculated echo" of Bécquer's *Rimas* I and VII.[12] Furthermore, Gilman also pointed out that Salinas, like Bécquer, set his poem in the form of a dialogue from the first to the second person, with the beloved appearing as an elusive or evasive recipient of the words.

Bécquer's *Rimas* also are said to have been inspired by a real love affair, and this fact must have been known to his contemporaries, since his well-meaning editors rearranged the manuscript of his collected verses in narrative sequence to conform with biographical details. Whatever the case may be, Bécquer concentrated less on the true reality of his beloved than on the symbolic value that her love held for him. The beloved woman performs several functions in the *Rimas*. She is at once the source and end of poetry, a poetic world complete in herself, and an unattainable ideal. This eclectic value has its origins in a prototype which began perhaps, with German Romanticism (and was continued also in Poe and Baudelaire, along paths similar to Bécquer's). Bécquer's literary example does indeed find an unmistakable echo in Salinas' poem, as we shall now see.

III   A *Paradise Lost*: The Voice Owed to You

The Voice Owed to You follows a circular narrative plan going from the discovery of love (a new reality), to plenitude of love (the creation of an earthly paradise), lost love (Paradise Lost), until the very last poem, which anticipates a recovery of lost happiness. Within this plan, the book could be divided into an Introduction and four parts. The Introduction (Nos. 1-2, verses 1-77)[13] is made up of the "proem" analyzed by Gilman, and the second poem, which is an invitation to the reader to follow the poet's path of a poetic discovery through love. In Part I (Nos. 2-3, verses 78-200), we witness the birth of love. In Part II, the plenitude of love, (Nos. 7-21, verses 201-830), a new paradisaical world is created and the roles of the beloved are defined. The climax of Part II with verses 700-830, ending with poems 20 and 21, which, according to González Muela, were intended to express Salinas' definition of love.[14] Part III goes from plenitude to separation. In this longest part, the relationship between the two lovers is inverted: whereas previously the woman was the guide in the rediscovery of reality, it is now the poet who assumes the role of "revealer" of his beloved's true essence. Salinas' lasting concern for the ambiguity of appearances reemerges in this part as the beloved becomes part of an impenetrable and shifting reality. Love is now an eternal questioning leading to incomprehension, spiritual separation, and finally, parting (Nos. 22-63, verses 831-2220).[15] Part IV: Paradise Lost. The poet examines the nature of love in the light of the corrosion of time. Several solutions are examined: Love as illusion, as Platonic ideal, and finally as eternal force, a soul constantly reincarnated in new generations of lovers (Nos. 64-70, verses 2220-2462).

Bearing in mind this organization, one can agree with J. Palley's statement on the poem's three basic directions: "*La voz a tí debida* is a long meditation on the reality of the beloved. It is a hymn in praise of the beloved. It represents the victory of love—being over nothingness."[16] Although the poem deals only with love, we shall see that Salinas' previous themes—poetry as discovery, the deceitfulness of appearances, inner vs. outer reality—also come into play.

The first motif is introduced in the "proem," where the woman's personality and her dominant role are established:

I

Tú vives siempre en tus actos. (You live forever by your actions.
Con la punta de tus dedos With the tips of your fingers
pulsas el mundo, le arrancas you strum on the world; it gives forth

auroras, triunfos, colores, [beautiful] dawns, triumphs, colors,
5 *alegrías: es tu música.* and joys: such is your music.
La vida es lo que tú tocas. Life is everything that you touch.

19 *Tú nunca puedes dudar.* You are never beset by doubt.
Porque has vuelto los misterios because you've turned all mysteries

del revés [........]	inside out. ....
30 *Y nunca te equivocaste,*	And you were never led astray
más que una vez, una noche	except once, on the night
que te encaprichó una sombra	that you flirted with a shadow
—la única que te ha gustado—	—the only one that ever pleased you—
Y la quisiste abrazar.	And trying to embrace it [you saw]
Y era yo. (pp. 219-20)	That it was I.)

What is immediately apparent in this young woman's nature is her boundless vitality, her self-sufficiency in creating her own circumstances, and her capacity not only for looking beyond ordinary reality, but for transforming it, "playing" on the world as if it were a musical instrument of unexpected melodious quality: *La vida es lo que tú tocas* (1. 6). By life, Salinas means of course existence already transformed by the imagination, discoverer of *"trasrrealidad."* The *amada's* life is, so to speak, a continuous poem.

Bécquer had written about his beloved, in *Rima* XXI, *Poesía eres tú* (You are poetry), meaning that she was at once poetic inspiration, poetic matter, and an instrument of perception which evoked sensibilities previously unknown to him. For Bécquer, the woman was also a guide leading him in his search for a mystical-pantheistic (Swendenborgian) ideal.

Salinas' beloved is also "poetry," but she does not lead him outside this world. The material world is the only reality on which she operates. C. Feal Deibe has pointed out that the three most important senses, touch, sight, hearing, come into play in the initial description of her,[17] making her a very tangible being who enjoys life to its fullest, in marked contrast with the poet himself who appears as a "shadow," still buried in a moribund routine world.

The initiation into love begins with a depurative process, at first slow and hesitating, one by which the poet must learn to abandon his predefined and conventional view of reality and direct himself to its rediscovery with the *amada* as a guide, conscious and fearful of his own limitations. Above all, he fears that the promised happiness will be only temporary and all the more deceitful if then lost:

VI
182 *Di, ¿podré yo vivir*   (Tell me, how shall I live
      en esos otros climas   in those new climates
      o futuros, o luces,   or futures, or lights,
      que estás elaborando [. . .]?   which you are inventing . . .?
186 *¿O seré sólo algo*   Or shall I be an object
      que nació para un día   born only for one of your
      tuyo (mi día eterno)?   days (my sole eternal day)?)
                      (p. 227)

There is briefly a temptation to abandon the promise of a real
happiness and to take refuge in an inner world of dreams which,
though a pale shadow of this new Spring, would at least be
permanent.

V
145 *No.*   (No.
      Tengo que vivirlo dentro,   I must live it within me
      me lo tengo que soñar.   I must dream it to myself.
153 *Y así, cuando se desdiga*   And if she ever should deny
      de lo que entonces me dijo,   the things she told me on that
                                                  day,
      no me morderá el dolor.   I will not feel the sting of pain.

159 *Creeré que fue soñado.*   I'll just believe it was a dream
      Que aquello, tan de verdad,   that all the things that seemed so
      no tuvo cuerpo, ni nombre.   real
                                              lacked both a body and a name.
      Que pierdo   That I'm losing
      una sombra, un sueño más.   a shadow, just another dream.)
                      (p. 225)

Soon, the poet abandons this cautious stand. Beginning with
the seventh poem, his verses reflect a steadily rising enthusiasm
for a world now seen through a sensibility transformed by love
and the beloved's contagious vitality:

VII
201 *"Mañana." La palabra*   ("Tomorrow." The word
      iba suelta, vacante,   moved freely, vacant,
      ingrávida, en el aire   weightless in the air
      tan sin alma y sin cuerpo,   so without soul and body, . . .
          [. . .]

208 *Pero de pronto tú*   But suddenly you
    dijiste: "Yo, mañana . . ."   said: "Tomorrow I . . ."
    Y todo se pobló   and everything was filled
    de carne y de banderas.   with banners and with flesh.
    Se me precipitaban   Promises
    encima las promesas   of six hundred colors
    de seiscientos colores, [. . .]   came rushing toward me, . . .
229 *¡Mañana! Qué palabra*   Tomorrow! What a word
    toda vibrante, tensa   of vibrance, now erect
    de alma y carne rosada,   in soul and rosy skin,
    cuerda del arco donde   the string of the bow on which
    tú pusiste, agudísima   you deftly placed the piercing
    arma de veinte años,   weapon of your twenty years,
    la flecha más segura   the most accurate arrow,
    cuando dijiste: "Yo . . ."   when you said: "I . . .")
                (pp. 229-30)

At this point, the plenitude of love is only a promise: "tomorrow." The first necessary transformation will be the shedding of circumstantial limitations. The very name of things must be forgotten. Even the name of love, since it is so often associated with too trivial sentiments, stands as a barrier to the full play of the deep poetic and emotional experience on which the poet is about to embark:

                IX
        285 *¿Por qué tienes nombre tú,*
            día, miércoles?
            ¿Por qué tienes nombre tú,
            tiempo, otoño?
            Alegría, pena, siempre
            ¿por qué tenéis nombre: amor?

        299 *Si tú no tuvieras nombre,*
            todo sería primero, [. . .]
        304 *Gozo, amor: delicia lenta*
            de gozar, de amar: sin nombre. (p. 233)

            (Why do you have a name;
            today's date, Wednesday?
            And you, why did they name you;
            time, autumn?

Happiness, sorrow, forever,
why do they call you love?

If only you were nameless
all things could start anew, . . .
Joy, love: languorous pleasure
of enjoying, of loving: without name.)

In this newly found bliss, with the *amada* to lead him, the poet first begins to free himself of the limitations of time, anticipating a world where present, past, and future will be abolished, or at least forgotten. The first quality of this new world will be its immutability, the eternal quality and instantaneous perfection of each moment:

XII
388 *Yo no necesito tiempo*   (I don't need any time
     para saber cómo eres;   to know you as you are;
     conocerse es el relámpago.   for knowing is like lightning.)
                  (p. 238)

At the same time, love and beloved are confused in this world where all sensations are accumulated, preserved, and directed toward ever greater perfection:

X
338 *Cuando te miré a los besos*   (As I looked at you through the
                                         virgin
     vírgenes que tú me diste,   kisses which you gave me,
     los tiempos y las espumas,   all times and all sea-foams,
     las nubes y los amores   the clouds and love conquests
     que perdí estaban salvados. I'd lost, were saved forever.)
                  (pp. 234-35)

The next section of Part II (Nos. 13-18, verses 425-700) contains the first allusions anticipating the genesis of an earthly paradise, center of the whole universe, and filled with the sole presence of the two lovers. Creation is preceded by the violent destruction of the past, symbolized by an enclosed temple (roofs, columns) darkened by the patina of time, and in which ordinary instruments of perception (weights, measures, numbers) have been stored for centuries of routine existence:

XVII

611 Amor, amor, catástrofe.

(Love, love, what a thundering crash

¡Qué hundimiento del mundo!

brings the world tumbling down!

Un gran horror a techos
quiebra columnas, tiempos;
los reemplaza por cielos
intemporales. Andas, ando
por entre escombros
de estíos y de inviernos
derrumbados. Se extinguen

A deep hatred for roofs
breaks down columns and times;
replacing them with timeless
heavens. I walk, you walk
stepping over the rubble
of summers and of winters,
now scattered ruins. Darkness falls

las normas y los pesos.
Toda hacia atrás la vida
se va quitando siglos,
frenética, de encima;
desteje, galopando,
su curso, lento antes;
se desvive de ansia
de borrarse la historia,
de no ser más que el puro
anhelo de empezarse
otra vez [. . .]

on measures and on weights.
Life on a backward course
is shedding centuries
in frenzy from itself;
unraveling at full speed
the course it once took slowly,
consumed by one desire:
to efface history,
to be only the pure
burning wish of beginning
life anew . . .

649 Y ya siento entre tactos
entre abrazos, tu piel
que me entrega el retorno
al palpitar primero
sin luz, antes del mundo,
total, sin forma, caos.[18]
(pp. 248-49)

And already I feel
in caresses, in embraces
your skin again evoking
the initial pulsation
in darkness, before the world,
total, formless, chaos.)

Out of this chaos, the new world will emerge,[19] as docile matter totally at the command of the lovers, The *amada*, who until now has had the role of guiding the poet out of darkness, now acts as "creator," justifying the description given of her in the "proem":

XIII

425 ¡Qué gran víspera el mundo!
No había nada hecho.
Ni materia, ni números,
ni astros, ni siglos, nada.

(Beautiful pre-world dawn!
Nothing had yet been made.
Neither matter, nor numbers,
or planets, or centuries, nothing.

480 *El gran mundo vacío*   The great empty world
    sin empleo, delante   lay unused before
    de ti estaba: su impulso   you: its impulse
    se lo darías tú.   would come from you.
    Y junto a ti, vacante,   And standing by your side, idle,
    por nacer, anheloso, [. . .]   yet to be born, anxiously, . . .
490 *yo, esperando*   I, hoping,

492 *a que tú me quisieses*   that only you should love me
    y me dijeras: "Ya."   and tell me: now.)
              (pp. 240-42)

We are beginning to see in these lines the emerging nature of this earthly paradise about to be born—earthly because the material world will not be excluded from it but merely redefined under the lover's scrutiny, and in a constant vital flux. The poet clearly attributes this transformation to the beloved's vitalizing presence, to the point that she is at once creator of this new reality and identified with the world she creates. She becomes *amada cósmica,* a motif which will be further accentuated in Part III of the poem, when, in order to recapture her lost presence, the poet recalls: *un jardín o tus labios/ con árboles, con besos* (2029, p. 311), (a garden, or your lips/ filled with trees and with kisses). Or in another poem, on the theme of evasion: *Empújame, lánzame/ desde ti, de tus mejillas,/ como islas de coral* (1139, p. 272), (Send me forth, launch me/ from you, from your cheeks/ as from coral islands). These two examples suffice to show that the world associated with the *amada* is evoked both as a Garden of Eden[20] and as a sea, complete in itself, yet never static, a motif which anticipates the poetry of *El contemplado.*

But this world, though not an immaterial Platonic circle, is a paradise, because it exists independently of ordinary material limitations. The lovers live in an eternal present and acquire new identity, known only to themselves, and symbolized only by pronouns more perfect and more intimate than nouns:

        XV
495 *Para vivir no quiero*   (To live I do not want
    islas, palacios, torres.   islands, palaces, towers.

¡Qué alegría más alta	Oh, what great joy it is
vivir en los pronombres!	to live only in pronouns!)
(p. 243)	

We are now close to the climax of *The Voice Owed to You* at the end of Part II. It is framed within three of the most jubilant poems in praise and definition of love. The first is directed to the *amada*. It is as if, like any lover, the poet cannot find the words to express his love, and falls back on the chaotic enumeration where feeling clearly surpasses all formal bounds:

XIX

702	¡Sí, todo con exceso:	(Yes, everything in superlatives:
	la luz, la vida, el mar!	light, life, and the sea!
	Plural todo, plural,	Plural, everything plural,
	luces, vidas y mares.	lights, lives and seas.
	A subir, a ascender	Let us rise, let us progress
	de docenas a cientos,	from dozens to hundreds,
	de cientos a millar,	from hundreds to thousands
	en una jubilosa	in a jubilant
	repetición sin fin,	and endless repetition
	de tu amor, unidad.	of your love: unity.
729	Y al otro lado ya	And already beyond
	de cómputos, de sinos,	calculations, or destinies,
	entregarnos a ciegas	let us blindly surrender
733	a un gran fondo azaroso	to a great chance adventure
	que irresistiblemente	which unrestrainably
	está	keeps
	cantándonos a gritos	singing to us aloud
	fúlgidos de futuro:	full of faith in the future:
	"Eso no es nada aún	"This joy is nothing yet;
	Búscaos bien, hay más."	deeper within yourselves there is more.")

(pp. 251-53)

The third poem is the most moving and should dispel once and for all the notion of a Salinas locked in a private Narcissistic world. The poem is about sharing, and it is clear that at the height of their love the poet is as necessary to his beloved as she is to him. They now live in a perfect union which distance, separation, and even death cannot destroy:

XXI
792 *Qué alegría, vivir*
sintiéndose vivido.
Rendirse
a la gran certidumbre, oscuramente,
de que otro ser, fuera de mí, muy lejos,
me está viviendo.

825 *Y todo enajenado podrá el cuerpo*
descansar, quieto, muerto ya. Morirse
en la alta confianza
de que este vivir mío no era sólo
mi vivir: era el nuestro. Y que me vive
otro ser por detrás de la no muerte. (pp. 256-57)

(What joy it is to live
feeling oneself being lived.
Surrendering
with blind trust, to the absolute conviction
that someone else, besides me, far from me,
is living my life.

Unmindful of its own reality, my body
will rest quietly, as good as dead. And yet, near death,
filled with the earnest confidence
that the life which I was living was not only
my life: that it was our possession. That someone else
is living me beyond a death that is not Death.)

Part II of *The Voice Owed to You* is the proclamation of
faith in life transformed by poetry and spontaneous feeling,
which we have seen as the driving force behind Salinas'
poetry since *Presages*. The message is always the same: keep
your eyes wide open to the marvels of the world, and be
prepared to embark without question in the adventure of each
new day: *hay que embarcarse en todos/ los proyectos que
pasan,/ sin preguntarles nada* (we must embark on every/
project which life parades before us/ and never ask any
questions), (vv. 766-68, p. 254). This was already the meaning
implied in "Water in the Night" and the related opening poems
of *Presages*. What awaits us is "steadfast chance": *el gran
fondo azaroso* ... But Love for the first time offers an ideal

and a tangible perfection which until now Salinas had not found.

The section of *The Voice Owed to You* just discussed contains some of the most beautiful love poetry ever written, but Part III is the most moving, as we witness the poet's desperate attempts to uphold this perfection, and to convince himself that it still exists, even when it is obvious that the lovers have already begun to drift apart. The poet can no longer maintain in his verses the intensity which characterized Part II. Instead, there is a constant movement between Love's presence, still sung in rapturous praise (e.g., No. 30, "Horizontal sí te quiero" ["Horizontal is how I want you"]), p. 271; or No. 38, "Qué entera cae la piedra" ("How heavily the stone does fall"), p. 281, and love's absence: love in the form of memories, dream, or illusion.

The beloved's self-reliance and her constantly changing perspectives on the world, which the poet can no longer share, are now seen as signs of frivolity. She is still the "pure living impulse," but she does not always live up to her fullest promise, and needs the poet to hold her to her "true" self.

The introduction of this motif marks the beginning of Part III, right in the first poem, which also initiates the theme of separation:

> XXII
> 831 *Afán*
>   *para no separarme*
>   *de ti, por tu belleza.*
>
> 845 *Y mientras siguen*
>   *dando vueltas y vueltas, entregándose,*
>   *engañándose,*
>   *tus rostros, tus caprichos y tus besos,*
>   *tus delicias volubles, tus contactos*
>   *rápidos con el mundo,*
>   *haber llegado yo*
>   *al centro puro, inmóvil, de ti misma,*
>   *Y verte cómo cambias*
>   *—y lo llamas vivir—*
>   *en todo, en todo, sí,*
>   *menos en mí, donde te sobrevives.* (p. 258)

(A struggle
not to be forced to part
from you, because of your beauty.

And [seeing], perpetually
caught in an aimless cycle of offering themselves,
and deceiving themselves,
your faces, your whims, your kisses,
your fickle charms, your casual
encounters with the world,
I have reached on my own
the pure immutable center of your inner self,
Watching as you go on changing
—though you call it living—
everything about you, in each and every way,
except within me, where you've gained your immortality.)

There are many poems of this kind, such as No. 34: "Lo
que eres/ me distrae de lo que dices" ("What you are/
distracts me from the words you say"). In No. 40: "¡Qué
probable eres tú!" ("How potential you are!"), the former
roles are clearly reversed and it is the *amada* who, guided
by the poet, must change from being *probable, criatura dudosa*
(potential and doubtful creature) to *irrefutable tú/ desnuda
Venus cierta* (irrefutable you, certain, naked Venus), vv.
1444-45, p. 284. (Later, in discussing Salinas' technique, I
shall analyze the poem which I consider to be the best and
most poignant of this series, No. 41, p. 285.) These are the
poems which, often read out of context, have, no doubt,
given rise to the idea that Salinas' *amada* is an abstract being,
and that her personality counts for very little beside the
concept and ideal that the poet maintains of her in his love-
dream.

In context, we see that these poems occur only after the
lovers already have lost the perfect harmony in which previously they would have acted, seen the world, and intuitively
known each other. Having lost this spiritual union, even
physical manifestations of love can become deceitful appearances. Kisses can be barriers: *Entre tu verdad más honda/
y yo/ me pones siempre tus besos* (Between your deepest
truth/ and me/ you keep interposing your kisses), vv. 1855-57,

p. 303. The beloved's forehead becomes a symbol of the distance between them (No. 54), and her skin becomes a disguise: ... *la piel/ disfraza levemente/ la defensa absoluta/ del ser último...* (your skin/ in a subtle disguise/ [is] the impregnable defense/ of your ultimate self...), vv. 1902-5, p. 304. To know each other is no longer a lightning process, but a tedious questioning and always repeated dialogue, now clearly anchored in time:

XLII

1471 *¿Hablamos, desde cuándo?* (How long have we been speaking?

¿Quién empezó? No sé. Who began? I don't know.
Los días mis preguntas; The days are my questions;
oscuras, anchas, vagas, obscure, [too] broad and vague,
tus respuestas: las noches. [and] your replies, the nights.

1491 *Los años y la vida* [Through] the years, and
                                                                [through] life
¡qué diálogo angustiado! what anguished dialogue!
Y sin embargo, And yet almost
por decir casi todo. all remains to be said.)
                    (p. 286)

It is in this context that the poet once again becomes skeptical of reality, including that of the beloved. Even as she stands before him, he may feel so completely estranged from her that she might as well be a mirror reflection (as in that other poem, No. 8 of *Pressages,* which I analyzed in the previous chapter):

XLIX

1747 *Tus espectros, qué brazos* (Spectres of you, with long
largos, qué labios duros arms, and hard lips,
tienen: sí, como tú. exactly as you have them.

[........] Yo vivo .... I live
de sombras, entre sombras from shadows, and among shadows

de carne tibia, bella of warm and beautiful flesh
con tus ojos, tu cuerpo, with your eyes, your body,
tus besos, sí con todo your kisses, with everything
lo tuyo, menos tú. (p. 297) that's yours without being you.)

The logical reaction is, as before, to take refuge in an inner world of dreams, more stable than reality. This is expressed in the verses which so disturbed many critics and prompted C. B. Morris to write that: "Salinas methodically amputated the woman's lips, destroyed her complexion...to live and love in a world free from the exciting but troublesome presence of the flesh":[21]

> XLVI
> 1946 *Me estoy labrando tu sombra.*
> *La tengo ya sin los labios,*
> *rojos y duros: ardían.*
>
> 1957 *Lo que más pena*
> *me ha dado, al callártela*
> *es tu voz. Densa, tan cálida*
> *más palpable que tu cuerpo.*
> *Pero iba a traicionarnos.* (p. 307)
>
> (I'm evoking your shadow to myself
> I've made it without lips. [They were
> so] red and hard, that they burned.
>
> What has grieved me
> most was parting with the sound
> of your voice. So tangible and warm
> more palpable even than your body.
> But [I knew] it would betray us.)

We have to understand these verses in the poet's present frame of mind, reflecting his loss and his sense of frustration at having been deceived, not as reflecting the mood of the entire poem. He himself will never be convinced that *tu solo cuerpo posible/ tu dulce cuerpo pensado* (your only possible body/ your soft imagined body), vv. 1980-81, p. 188, will in the end be a substitute for real life. This attitude of escape from reality is for Salinas only temporary, and he will soon explore new ways out of his dilemma.

By the end of Part III, the separation is complete between the lovers. No. 60 is a poem to tears, as symbolic of the eternal mystery of love:

LX

2106 *¡Qué gusto negro y denso*   (What a dark and thick taste
     a tierra, a sol, a mar!   of the earth, of the sun, and the
                              sea!

2115 *¿Son estrellas, son signos,*   Are they stars, are they symbols,
     son condenas o auroras?   condemnations, or dawnings?
     Ni en mirar ni en besar   Neither in seeing or kissing
                              [them]
     aprendí lo que eran.   did I discover what they were.)
          (p. 314)

No. 63 shows the poet's desperate clinging to memories, even
to pain, as the last vestige of his lost love:

LXIII

2191 *No quiero que te vayas,*
     dolor, última forma
     de amar. Me estoy sintiendo
     vivir cuando me dueles [. . .]

2213 *tú me serás, dolor, [. . .]*

2216 *La gran prueba, a lo lejos,*
     de que existió, que existe,
     de que me quiso, sí
     de que aún la estoy queriendo. (p. 319)

(I don't want you to leave me,
sorrow, ultimate form
of love. I feel that I am
alive only when you hurt me . . .

for me—O sorrow—you will be

The ultimate and distant proof
that she existed, and still exists,
that she loved me, yes,
and that I still love her.)

It is no wonder that as his book contains poems of such
emotional depth, Salinas himself should have been shocked—

as J. Guillén tells us[22]—by Spitzer's interpretation of *The Voice Owed to You* as dry conceptualization.

Only six poems remain, forming the fourth and final "act" of *The Voice Owed to You*. In a sense, we may consider Part IV as a prelude to *Love's Reason*. These poems are meditations on the nature of love once the actual experience has ended, as most of the next book also will be.

IV *Paradise Regained*: Love's Reason

Although *Love's Reason* was published three years after *The Voice Owed to You,* it cannot be regarded as a totally new book, and it would be difficult to understand its meaning and imagery fully without the preparation which occurred in the first part of the cycle.

On the narrative level, the book makes allusions to the love experience now totally ended, and which the poet strives to justify and recapture, not in real life—where it could again be lost—but in a more durable and meaningful realm. What he attains in the end is both a personal solution and the basis for a whole philosophy of life founded on love. For this reason, the title of the book should perhaps more aptly be translated as *Love's Purpose*.[23] On the symbolic level, some of the motifs introduced in *The Voice Owed to You* are continued and ultimately resolved in the new book.

The overall plan of *Love's Reason* is less apparent than that of *The Voice Owed to You*. Salinas indicated two parts and chose to give titles to the eight poems which make up Part II. These poems thus stand out more. They are also considerably longer than any previously included in either book, yet they contain no new theme or motif. Part II could be viewed as a final summary of arguments put forth in defense or justification of love.

Part I might further be divided into two sections. The first (Nos. 1-31. vv. 1-1438, pp. 335-59) connects clearly with *The Voice Owed to You,* elaborating further on the myth of the Garden of Eden, now closed to the lovers (e.g., vv. 121-24, p. 340; or 355-61, p. 349), and introducing with more insistence the possibility of a "redemption" (No. 4, especially the ending,

vv. 197-200, p. 343). In this section, a positive view of love alternates with a sense of nostalgia and loss. For example, the first poem is in praise of love as creator of light, but the second proclaims that from its first moment of inception love was already an inevitable parting. Numbers 3 and 4 are "positive" poems. The first offers the consolation that even if paradise is negated, life will be made richer in its search; the second again praises the beloved as "tamer of miracles" and as guide, even in absence. But in No. 5 (p. 344), we have again a "negative" view. Love is an obscure force desperately seeking new incarnations and being offered only dreams to satiate its desires.

This opening section of *Love's Reason* also contains some rather mediocre poems (e.g., No. 14, p. 360; No. 16, p. 365), and some so involved in conceptual subtleties as to obscure feeling (No. 12, p. 357, especially the first two verses). However, beginning with No. 32, p. 393 (or perhaps even in the four or five preceding poems),[24] the text regains an intensity matching that of *The Voice Owed to You*. New imagery is introduced, based on the symbolism of water and the sea, and surrounding the motif of salvation or "paradise regained." In my discussion, I shall insist more on these later poems, in which the means toward salvation are defined, and on those of Part II. I shall present each theme in order of increasing importance, but not necessarily following the order in which it is introduced in the book.

The first lasting value of love, as is to be expected with Salinas, is the new "perspective" that it has given him on the world. Even though the *amada* is no longer with him, the poet will never be alone because she has taught him to see the world through her eyes. The *amada* now appears as the "soul" of all things, present in all things. Once more, we are reminded of Bécquer and of the Symbolists' *correspondances*:

XXX
1357 *Ahora marchas, lo sé,*   (I know that you are departing
a infinita distancia,   for an infinitely distant land,
pero laten tus pasos   but your steps still resound
en todas esas vagas   in all those vague and
sombras de ruido, tenues,   tenuous shadows of sound,

que en la alta noche estre-   reverberating in the depth of
llan   night
el azul del silencio: on the blue [screen] of silence:
todas suenan a ecos.   sounds which all seem like echoes.

1378 Todo sonido en eco   My soul awaiting [you]
      tuyo me lo convierte   perceives in every sound
      el alma que te espera.   an echo from your voice.

1387 Se te vio en tu marchar   And your departure seemed
      el revés: tu venida,   just the opposite: a new presence
      vibrante en el adiós.   vibrating in your parting words.
      Igual que vibra el alba   As the light of dawn vibrating
      en el gris, en el rosa,   in the gray and pink colors
      que pisando los cielos,   moving across the skies
      con paso de crepúsculo,   with the procession of dusk
      al acabar el día   marking the end of day,
      parecen—y son ella,   might seem—although it is
      la que viene, inminente—   the imminent nascent light—
      una luz que se va.   a light which is departing.)
           (pp. 392-93)

The poet no longer lives in the world, but in her *traspresencia,*
or *trasrrealidad*: the new associations with which she has imbued
even the most trivial things:

        XXXVII
  1610 Tan convencido estoy
        de tu gran traspresencia [. . .]

  1615 que no estoy nunca solo
        mientras la luz del día me parece tu alma. (p. 403)

        (I feel so utterly imbued
        with your magnificent real presence . . .

        that I shall never be alone
        while daylight seems the radiance of your soul.)

In turn, the world, and all things in the world, reinterpreted
through poetry will forever be the irrefutable proof of his
great love for her:

XXXVII

1637 *Si te quiero*
no es porque te lo digo:
es porque me lo digo y me lo dicen [. . .]

1649 *las músicas casuales que se encuentran*
al abrir los secretos de la noche. (p. 404)

(I love you
not because I tell you so
but because I tell myself, and I'm told by all . . .

the harmonies so casually revealed
upon divulging the night's secrets.)

The first victory of love, then, is to have brought the poet out of himself and into contact with another sensibility, widening his experience in so doing. In turn, the lovers have acquired a collective "Truth of Two" (see No. 40, p. 383), a unique perspective which is theirs alone but which will be assimilated by future generations of lovers, presumably through poetry.[25] For love is an eternal cyclic force, always repeated and yet never reincarnated in exactly the same way. This idea gives love the eternal quality which Salinas previously sought in vain, and, at the same time, it gives lovers immortality and a justification on the basis of each individual experience:

XXXIX

1663 *Ellos ¿Los ves, dí, los*   (Tell me, do you see them and
    sientes?   feel
   Están hechos de nosotros,   [that] they are made only from
    [. . .]   us?

1671 *ellos*   they're [just]
   somos nosotros querién-   ourselves still loving one another.
    donos, [. . .]

1674 *Lo que fuimos lo que somos*   What we once were, and what
                       we are,
   ¡qué empezar torpe, tan   what an awkward beginning
    sólo,
   qué tanteo entre tinieblas,   and haphazard progression in
                       darkness

hacia lo que ellos serán!	toward their future realization!
1680 *Vivir es vivirse en ellos.*	To live on is to live without them.
1683 *[. . .] esas imágenes viejas,*	. . . those tired and ancient images
usadas de ti y de mí	of you and me
—lo que somos—	—[are] what we are now—
nosotros vamos, arriba,	[but] steadily we are ascending,
hechos ellos, por lo alto,	taking their form, in the highest realm,
flotando en el paraíso	floating in the paradise
de lo que anhelamos ser.	of all the things we wished to be.)
(p. 405)	

The paradise which is regained is not a private world as
before, but the great sum of love experiences, past and future,
adequately symbolized by the sea: *el gran querer callado, mar
total* (the great silent love, the total sea), v. 1662, p. 404.)
The sea is complete in itself and immutable, always repeated
in the eternal joining and parting of waves, yet never the
same.[26] The sea collects the waters of all rivers. Therefore, if
the sea represents the ultimate and unchanging perfection, the
river, and in general flowing water, stands for a future promise:
the movement of all lives and of Nature toward their harmonious fulfillment in the sea.

XXIX

1235 *Mundo de lo prometido,*	(A world filled with promises
agua.	[in the] water.
Todo es posible en el agua.	All things made possible through the water.
1238 *[. . .] el mundo que está detrás*	. . . the world which hides behind [all things]
en el agua se me aclara.	is suddenly made clearer in the water.
1244 *La montaña [. . .]*	The mountain . . .
. . . .	
1246 *se me enternece en lo verde*	lures me with gentler shapes in the green
líquido, rompe cadenas,	liquidness, having broken its bonds,

se escapa,	it is escaping,
dejando atrás su esqueleto,	leaving behind its empty skeleton;
ella fluyente, en el agua.	it is flowing by, in the water.

1286 *De recta que va, de alegre,*	And as the water flows, directly and
el agua hacia su destino,	happily toward its destiny,
el terror de lo futuro	all our fears of the future
en su ejemplo se desarma:	will be disarmed by its example:
si ella llega, llegaremos,	if it reaches the goal, so shall we,
ella, nosotros, los dos,	—both of us, and the water—reach
al gran término del ansia.	the great fulfillment of our longing.)

(pp. 387-88)

It is only in the light of this poem, and of similar ones in *Love's Reason* (see also No. 36, p. 402, especially the last two verses) that we understand the full significance of some of Salinas' earlier poems, from "Water in the Night" in *Presages*, to "The Friars' Garden" in *Fable and Signs*, as well as in some of the later poetry in *All Things Made Clearer*. We see to what amazing degree Salinas' works form a whole, and also, how his concept of poetry—always expanding, on the same dynamic basis, toward greater clarity and perfection—is parallel to his conception of love.

Part II of *Love's Reason* summarizes and further clarifies the idea of salvation through love. The first poem: "Salvación por el cuerpo" ("Salvation Through the Flesh"), p. 419, is a sort of epic of man from birth to his immortal condition in paradise regained. First we see the incarnation of a soul into a new body, then the adolescent's first sensual discovery of this body:

1971 *[....................] Un día,*
la infatigable sed de ser corpóreo
en nosotros irrumpe,
lo mismo que la luz, necesitada
de posarse en materia para verse,
por el revés de sí, verse en su sombra.

1981 *[....................] Nuestro cuerpo*

es el cuerpo primero en que vivimos,
y eso se llama juventud a veces. (p. 420)

(. . . . . One day
an insatiable longing for a corporeal
existence takes hold of us.
As with light so greatly in need of embracing
a material shape in order to see itself
present in its counterpart; reflected in its shadow.

. . . . Our own body
the first body through which we experience
the living joy which we sometimes call youth.)

Then one day, the perfect union of a body with another is
another step toward even greater sensorial enjoyment of the
world:

2033 *[. . .] cuerpo con cuerpo igual que agua con agua,*
corriendo juntos entre orillas
que se llaman los días más felices! (p. 422)

(one body joined with another as water is joined with water
both running their course between the banks
which we call our happiest days!)

But the final perfection is attained only within the collective
sea of love, the eternal body where all lovers finally find their
recompense:

2064 *[. . .] para encontrar, al cabo, al otro lado,*
su cuerpo, el del amor, último y cierto.
Ese
que inútilmente esperarán las tumbas. (p. 423)

(Finally, to encounter beyond the last frontier,
the ultimate and true body of Love.
That body
which the tomb will always claim in vain.)

The idea of a collective happiness, superior to any individual
fulfillment, is also the theme of the next poem: "El despertar"

("Awakening"), p. 424, and of "Suicidio hacia arriba" ("Suicide Toward Greater Heights"), p. 440. "El dolor" ("Suffering"), p. 427, offers love as a shield against its opposite: destruction or gratuitous [absurd] suffering.

"Destino alegre" and "Verdad de dos" ("Happy Destiny," p. 430, and "Truth of Two," p. 433) add the idea of the responsibility of each man to reconcile within his life the errant "souls" which continually wage their battle in the world:

"Destino alegre"

2292 *[. . .] madres de bien y de mal,*
malditas y benditas, hierro y pluma,
alba y desolación, duras hermanas,
que no pueden matarse y que se odian,
eternamente unidas:
tú, tú felicidad, tú, tú desgracia. (p. 431)

(. . . begetters of good and evil,
blessed and damned, made of steel or feathers,
of bright hope and despair, these cruel sisters
who cannot kill each other but fiercely hate
each other, eternally united:
Thou, happiness, and thou, affliction.)

Lovers take upon themselves, perhaps at the sacrifice of their individual happiness, the mission of "redeeming" the world (and with this theme, the biblical motif is completed), helpless prey of these antagonal forces, and restoring it to its full beauty:

2317 *el mundo sin oficio, puro, limpio,*
tendría que asumir el gran deber
humano: ser feliz, quererlo ser,
o recibir desgracia.
2325 *Nosotros le salvamos, en nosotros,*
al recibir, con los ojos cerrados,
la gran consagración llamada dicha,
o su hermana fatal. (p. 432)

(the pure, the clean, innocent world
would find weighing upon itself the great duty
of man: to be happy, to desire happiness,

or to withstand misfortune.
We shall save it within ourselves
by accepting, with closed eyes
the sacred fulfillment called joy,
or its perfidious sister.)

"Fin del mundo" ("End of the World"), p. 436, repeats the
theme of love as necessarily destructive of a banal world, while
the last poem, "La felicidad imminente" ("Imminent Happiness"), p. 440, is Salinas' personal proclamation of faith in life,
containing much the same message as *"Cara a Cara,"* the last
poem of Guillén's *Cántico.* Happiness is fullness of life and
acceptance of reality regardless of what may come, joy or
sorrow:

> 2692 *Escogido estoy ya para la hazaña*
> *del gran gozo del mundo:*
> *de soportar la dicha, de entregarla*
> *todo lo que ella pide, carne, vida,*
> *muerte, resurrección, rosa, mordisco;* [. . .] (p. 445)
>
> (I have been chosen to carry on the conquest
> of the great joy of the world:
> to withstand happiness and give it
> everything it demands, a body, a life,
> death, and resurrection, rose or bite . . .)

Man is necessary to incarnate the errant soul of happiness:

> 2728 *Me necesita para ser dichosa,*
> *lo mismo que a ella yo.*
>
> 2734 *[. . .] porque soy necesario a su gran ansia*
> *de ser*
> *algo más que la idea de su vida;*
>
> 2752 *Viva, ser viva, el algo humano quiere*
> *[. . . . .] Así se calma*
>
> 2767 *un instante su furia. Y ser felices*
> *es el hacernos campos de sus paces.* (pp. 446-48)

(It needs me to be conscious of its own joy
as I myself need it.

. . . because I'm needed to fulfill its great longing
to be
something other than the idea of its existence;

To live, to be alive, it yearns for a human complement
. . . . Only thus can

its fury momentarily be at peace. For us to be happy
is only to offer ourselves
as the battlefields where its peace is regained.)

Such is the conclusion drawn from Salinas' great love cycle. It is not that of an abstract idealist, an existentialist, or a Neoplatonist, but of a man very much of this world, accepting its imperfections, and optimistically making the best of his earthbound condition.

V *Style and Technique in* The Voice Owed to You

By the time he wrote *The Voice Owed to You,* Salinas had left behind the experimentations of the Vanguardist years and adopted a style which we now recognize as unmistakably his own. I have mentioned in passing some of the stylistic peculiarities of each of the first three books, but in the light of the poetry just discussed I can now point out some of the more permanent characteristics which contribute to Salinas' originality and poetic greatness. As with all the members of his literary generation, we will see that this style makes use of both traditional and very modern features.

Although *The Voice Owed to You* and *Love's Reason* are composed entirely of unrhymed verses, and often combine short and long meters in a single poem, they are not written in what is generally referred to as free verse. Anyone familiar with Spanish versification will recognize that Salinas used only traditional meters, and that even the combinations are not new.

Up to *The Voice Owed to You,* the favorite medium is the eight-syllable, very symetrically accented verse predominant in Spanish popular poetry and in the ballads, but from which Salinas has eliminated all but vague echoes of assonantal rhymes (and even these used only rarely). Octosyllabic verses are still very much in evidence in *The Voice Owed to You,* and even more in *Love's Reason,* especially in meditative poems for which its regular cadence is particularly suited. In *The Voice Owed to You,* however, Salinas mostly uses the Renaissance seven-syllabled verse, either alone or in combination with verses of eleven, or less frequently nine, syllables, and with *enjambements* of three to five syllables.

These combinations, especially the 7-11, had been used in Spain by classical poets such as San Juan de la Cruz and Fray Luis de León. Fray Luis was also very fond of *enjambements* which he put to very original uses. In his *Oda X:* "To Felipe Ruiz," we find for example the following verses: *Veré las immortales/ columnas do la tierra está fundada* (I shall see the immortal/ columns upon which the earth stands), which sound very much like Salinas.[27] I am not bent on proving a direct influence, but certainly there is a definite "echo" of Fray Luis's serene and elegant style in the poetry of our very modern poet.

Also very much in evidence in *The Voice Owed to You* is the whole Petrarchian tradition of love poetry, especially in the use of parallel constructions and images, and antagonistic elements. But, as in the case of popular tradition, Salinas adopted classical models while disregarding rhyme schemes entirely. He did not want to call attention to the music of rhymes, but to a more subtle internal cadence. Salinas is indeed a modern poet, and a characteristic which J. Maritain points out as one of the main innovations of the poetry of our time is strikingly evident with Salinas:

... Modern poetry had to dispense ... with the necessity of rhyme and the other requirements of classical prosody. Modern poetry is bound to obey more exacting laws and rules, for they are free and contingent rules, depending at each moment on the correctness of the ear, and on the fact of each and every word, measure and period in the poem being exactly in tune with the soundless music stirred by poetic intuition within the soul.[28]

What particularly distinguishes Salinas from his models, then, is the free displacement of accents within each verse, to create this internal rhythm, paralleling emotional surges within the poem, and reinforced by a very particular use of *enjambement.*

After *Fable and Sign,* Salinas seldom used complicated metaphors. In *The Voice Owed to You,* his images are mostly tied to a symbolic structure, such as the love-paradise or world-woman motifs. Single images tend not to be visual—as, for example, those of Lorca are—but conceptual, dealing with a reality of the mind rather than that of the world outside. Frequently, Salinas "concretizes" abstractions. Such is the case with the personification of Happiness, in one of the two poems I shall analyze, or in the description of the beloved's essence (real self) as if it were a real object, in the second poem to be discussed below.

Salinas continues to be fond of playing on the various meanings of one word, and of paradoxes. He uses neologisms: *traspresencia, reciennaciéndose, trasvivirse.* Another peculiar stylistic feature is the substantivization of pronouns, verbs, and even prepositions, or adverbs: *mi alma...toda afilada de quieros;* (my soul...all bristling with I love you's), *se anda a tu lado . . . tropezando en acasos . . .* (one walks by your side...on perhapses). Punctuation is always important for Salinas, both in maintaining a rhythm or, in the case of exclamation points, to set a mood. C. Feal Deibe has noted that many of the poems of *The Voice Owed to You* begin with an exclamation for dramatic effect (action and excitement), while in *Love's Reason* an interrogation often sets the meditative mood.[29]

I have chosen two poems, both taken from *The Voice Owed to You,* for analysis. The first, No. 15, p. 244, belongs to Part II, in the early stages of the discovery of love. The feeling expressed is one of happiness, not yet secure, accompanied by the fear that it will be merely a passing and fragile joy. The poet personifies Happiness, and pictures it as a display of fireworks, soaring to the sky, burning with intense fire and light, illuminating the world with order and beauty, but in a short time it ends up in smoke. The poem, up to verse 552, follows an ascending arc, then begins a downward movement, like a perfect ellipse:

522 *De prisa, la alegría*   (This happiness, bursting with
                                                   speed,

atropellada, loca.   impetuous and wanton.
Bacante disparada   A Bacchante swiftly soaring;
525 *del arco más casual*   shot out of some random bow
contra el cielo y el suelo.   against the heavens and the earth.
La física, asustada,   Startled, the laws of physics
tiene miedo; los trenes   are struck with awe; the trains
se quedan más atrás   are losing ground, remaining
530 *aún que los aviones*   even further behind the planes
y que la luz. Es ella,   or light itself. It is a joy
velocísima, ciega   that moves swiftly. A joy blind
de mirar, sin ver nada,   from gazing, without seeing,
y querer lo que ve.   desiring all it sees.
535 *Y no quererlo ya.*   Then no longer wanting it.
Porque se desprendió   Because it has abandoned
del quiero, del deseo,   all wish and desire,
y ebria toda en su esencia,   drunk with its own essence,
no pide nada, no   it requires nothing.
540 *va a nada, no obedece*   It goes nowhere. It heeds no
a bocinas, a gritos,   signal-horns, nor shouts,
a amenazas. Aplasta   nor warning threats. Trampling
bajo sus pies ligeros   underneath its winged feet
la paciencia y el mundo.   all patience, and the world itself.
545 *Y lo llena de ruinas*   It leaves it in a disarray
—órdenes, tiempo, penas—   —of [vain] commands, of times,
                                                   of sorrows—

en una abolición   in a triumphant and total
triunfal, total, de todo   abolition, of everything
lo que no es ella, pura   that is not itself; purest
550 *alegría, alegría*   happiness, the noble and mighty
altísima, empinada   happiness, raised on tiptoe,
encima de sí misma.   standing [triumphantly] upon it-
                                                   self.

Tan alta de esforzarse,   From such sustained effort, it
                                                   soared so high
que ya se está cayendo,   that it is already falling,
555 *doblada como un héroe,*   like a hero with head bent low
sobre su hazaña inútil.   confronting his useless exploit.
Que ya se está muriendo   It feels itself already dying,
consumida, deshecha   being consumed and dissolved
en el aire, perfecta   in mid-air, in the perfect
560 *combustión de su ser.*   holocaust of its being.

Y no dejará humo,	It will leave behind neither smoke,
ni cadáver, ni pena	nor body, nor regret
—memoria de haber sido—	—no memory of having been.
Y nadie la sabrá,	No one will recall it, no one,
565 *nadie, porque ella sola*	because this joy could only know
supo de sí. Y ha muerto.	about itself alone. And now it's dead.)

522-526

In a nervous rhythm, set off with punctuation, short phrases are launched like so many arrows in the sky. A series of nouns and adjectives are introduced, all indicating speed and impetuosity, but also carelessness and lack of planning. This is the first description of happiness, reinforced in the third verse by its personification as a beautiful, but foolish bacchante. The next two verses describe a projectile in midair, tracing a harmonious arch between heaven and earth, two antagonistic elements competing for its apex: *cielo, suelo* (sky, ground). The similarity of sound between these two words calls the reader's attention to the missile's lack of direction by equating the two forces. Happiness lacks a goal and could go either way.

527-531

The second personification of an abstraction is introduced; in this case, the laws of physics, suddenly afraid of this impetuous force which seems to defy all known measure of speed, represented here, in ascending order, by trains, planes, and the speed of light. All are thrusting themselves aside to avoid competition with the new victor.

531-552

The next five verses express a typical Salinian paradox, rendered in a rapid succession of contradictions, and by the use of *enjambement* in 532-533. The impetuous force of love-happiness, once it is reaching its climax, consumes itself in misdirected efforts. It is blind . . . from striving to see (not understanding what it sees); bursting with emotion, but frustrated in its desire for possession of the loved object. A movement from decisiveness to doubt is repeated no less than three times in five verses, in parallel series of antagonistic words: *velocísima, mirar, querer* vs. *ciega, sin ver nada, no quererlo ya.* The essential flaw of this happiness (caused by this first encounter with love) is that it is content with burning itself up in its own ecstatic joy, without asking anything of the future, in spite of warnings from the laws of a pragmatic world which proclaim in vain that all effort must seek a purpose and its ultimate realization.

We now witness the temporary victory of unabashed gratuitous feeling over reason, monotony, and routine. In the last three verses (550-552), all movement has stopped for an instant of static beauty of happiness in its apex, straining in its will to survive. On the level of sound, this is rendered in successive words by the insistence on the vowel *i* which helps to give the word *alegría* all its surging force: *alegría, altísima . . . encima de sí misma.*

553-566

Again, Salinas uses a paradox to signify the inner flaw of this blind force, already dying, though still almost at the peak of its strength, like an athlete who in spite of redoubled efforts sees that he will not win the race. The rhythm, now progressively slower, follows the trailing firecracker, which is paying dearly in self-combustion for an instant of triumph. Again, the *enjambement* (559-560) accentuates this plight by calling attention to the paradox of a triumphant destruction: *perfecta combustión.*

The rest of the poem introduces the idea of oncoming death and oblivion. Happiness was so fragile and illusory that it will leave behind neither body nor memory, or even smoke. It was a solitary and selfish happiness (not yet true love) which fulfilled itself in narcissistic contemplation. Since it was not directed toward another being, it could not be saved.

The construction of a poem along geometrical lines (ellipse or circle) is a typical feature of *The Voice Owed to You,* especially in the second and third parts. By contrast, in the section corresponding to the plenitude of love, we find poems proceeding in a straight line, and reaching their climax with the last verse (e.g., Nos. 19, p. 252, and 20, 21).

The second poem to be analyzed is from Part III (No. 41, p. 285). It is also constructed on a double movement, in this case first descending, then rising, as an inverted ellipse. The previous poem was all in seven-syllable verses, but in this one we find a combination of eleven-, seven-, four-, and three-syllabled lines.

The poem deals with the speaker's new role as discoverer of the beloved's "true essence," and as guiding light toward the lovers' greater fulfillment. On the emotional level, it first expresses the pain caused by incomprehension between the lovers, but this is resolved in a feeling of reconciliation and mutual understanding. Salinas has expressed these feelings above all with sound, and rhythm:

> *Perdóname por ir así buscándote*
> 1450 *tan torpemente, dentro*
> *de ti.*
> *Perdóname el dolor, alguna vez.*
> *Es que quiero sacar*
> *de ti tu mejor tú*
> 1455 *Ese que no te viste y que yo veo,*
> *nadador por tu fondo, preciosísimo.*
> *Y cogerlo*
> *y tenerlo yo en alto como tiene*
> *el árbol la luz última*
> 1460 *que le ha encontrado al sol.*
> *Y entonces tú*
> *en su busca vendrías, a lo alto.*
> *Para llegar a él*
> *subida sobre ti, como te quiero,*
> 1465 *tocando ya tan sólo a tu pasado*
> *con las puntas rosadas de tus pies,*
> *en tensión todo el cuerpo, ya ascendiendo*
> *de ti a ti misma.*
> *Y que a mi amor entonces le conteste*
> 1470 *la nueva criatura que tú eras.*

> (Forgive me for the ways I have of prying
> so clumsily, inside
> of you.
> Forgive the pain I cause you on occasion.
> It's just that I want to draw out

your best self from within yourself.
A you unsuspected by you, but which I see
like a swimmer sounding your very
                    precious depths.
I want to grasp it
and hold it up very high like
a tree conserving the last rays
which it drew from the sun.
Finally you
would come searching to the top.
Desiring to reach it
raised upon yourself, as I love you [best];
only barely touching your past
with the rosy tips of your feet,
and with your whole body tensely striving,
                    and already rising
from you to yourself.
Then let my love for you be greeted
by this newborn being that was always you.)

1449-1456

The irregular rhythm of the four initial verses follows exactly
the emotional thrust of a clumsy and hesitant search, full of
obstacles, into the private guarded world of the beloved. A
feeling of syncopation is obtained by an irregular pattern of
accentuation (the first verse has three *main* accents, the last
two following each other closely because of the antepenulti-
mate stress in the last word, and reinforced by the harsh repe-
tition of the *t* and *d* sounds, *tan tórpemente dentro de ti,* as
if each letter represented one more act of painful prodding.

The *enjambement* (1450-1451) has the function of further
breaking up the rhythm, and also of isolating the words *de ti*
to indicate the end of this deep penetration into the *amada*'s
inner soul. This private world is symbolized by watery depths
in which the speaker moves about like a deep-sea diver.

1457-1460

Having found the hidden treasure of her "true essence," the
diver surfaces again. These four verses show a steady ascent
toward sunlight, deliberately not mentioned until the end of
the fourth verse. The rhythm is no longer syncopated, but still

meandering, while the ascent is slowed by a second *enjambe-ment* (1459) also having the effect of drawing the reader's attention to a new, unexpected simile: that of a tree illuminated by the last rays of a crepuscular sun. This image may well seem out of place in the context of the poem, but it does present a vivid picture of a dazzlingly beautiful, yet fragile, treasure.

1461-1470

In the last part of the poem (1461-70), we see a second ascension, that of the *amada*, attracted by this new light. We should observe however, that the first verb is in the conditional tense, indicating the wish of the poet to play his new role of "revealer" rather than the beloved's actual compliance with this wish. These verses portray her steady course by the use of a measured rhythm, carefully set off with commas. We note some typical Salinian imagery, purely conceptual in nature. Salinas presents concepts and abstractions as if they were of a concrete nature. Both the *amada*'s "superficial self," and her past, are pictured as a ledge on which she is able to stand on tiptoe to reach upward toward the coveted object: her "true self." Verse 1468 also plays with syntax, since in Spanish the word *mismo* as used in this sentence should merely reinforce the prepositional object (as also in English: "you yourself"). But Salinas uses the two pronouns: *ti* and *ti misma* as if they designated two separate entities: a frivolous self and the beloved's potentially perfect self.

The last two verses of the poem resolve all tension with the harmonious reunion of the lovers. But the last word contains an ultimate paradox in the use of a past tense: *eras*. With this one word, Salinas reminds us of his faith in the perfectibility of man through love. The beloved's perfection was nothing new, but was always potentially there and needed only to be actualized by the lovers' altruistic feeling for each other.

CHAPTER 5

The Song Owed to Life:
(The Contemplated Sea, All Things
Made Clearer, Confidence)

I *From Individual to Collective Self-Realization*

IN *Love's Reason* we have seen that Salinas progressively acquired a new vital perspective, a sense of purpose, and accrued faith in the importance of his poetic mission. Until then, his poetry shows that he had been unable to find in the material world the measure of permanence which might help to give it meaning. If all things with which man came in contact were irrevocably doomed to destruction, and with individual existence necessarily rooted in the irreversible flux of time with death as its ending, life, however beautiful and enjoyable, could have no ultimate meaning; it was no better than a cruel illusion. We have seen that this conclusion is implicit throughout Salinas' first period. There is little evidence that he ever had a strong religious faith or any belief in values outside the material world of which he felt himself to be an intrinsic part. Therefore, his metaphysical skepticism should logically have led him to despair or to rebellion. But we have also seen that such an attitude was contrary to his basically optimistic inclination.

The intense experience related in *The Voice Owed to You* opened the poet's eyes and heart to a solution in harmony with this instinctive optimism. Although he remained exclusively a lay thinker, his philosophy of life followed a direction curiously parallel with that of two of the best-known contemporary theologians. Points of contact with the thought of Martin Buber, as expressed in his *I and Thou,* have been documented with pertinent quotes in Alma de Zubizarreta's study on Salinas.[1]

But the similarity with theories expounded by the Jesuit anthropologist-theologian Pierre Teilhard de Chardin are even more remarkable. One should not think in terms of influences, although Juan Marichal—Salinas' son-in-law and his major editor —tells us that the poet became an enthusiastic admirer of Teilhard's works in the last years of his life. Marichal points out the similarity and then makes use of Teilhard's terminology to explain the progression of Salinas' spiritual growth.[2]

For Teilhard, biological evolution reached its peak with man and was replaced with psychic evolution. Man became separated from other animals by his propensity for self-reflection. This concentration on the discovery of man's own self was then the point of departure toward an ever greater perfection which is still in progress. Each individual life, as well as all human life, progresses toward full maturity in three steps: (1) Full awareness of one's own self; (2) With the ability to love, the transferrence of the center of importance on a being other than oneself; (3) Fusion with an entity greater than oneself (the Omega point, at the conclusion of evolution, which for Teilhard is, of course, communion with God).[3]

It is easy to see how Salinas' first two periods could be viewed as the initial two stages of this spiritual evolution. However, I do not fully agree with Professor Marichal's rather negative evaluation of Salinas' first works as only tentative and groping for meaning.[4] In the previous chapters, we have seen to what remarkable degree Salinas' later development (both ideologically and in his choice of key images such as the water-symbol) was foreshadowed from *Presages* onward.[5]

In stage three, the definition of a collective reality and a collective, as opposed to individual, fulfillment at the end of the love cycle became from then on Salinas' unwavering preoccupation, as reflected at least in all the poetry written after 1939.

II   *Thematic Unity in Salinas' Late Poetry*

In my earlier classification of Salinas' works, I noted in passing that the three books of poetry included in this last period seemed strikingly different in mood. *El contemplado*

(*The Contemplated Sea*), 1946, is a song of near-mystic union with nature symbolized by the Caribbean Sea. It was written during two particularly happy years which Salinas spent as a visiting professor at the University of Puerto Rico (1943-1945). Salinas was relieved to find himself once more surrounded with his own Hispanic culture, after several years of residence in the United States. In Puerto Rico, he renewed old acquaintances among Spanish exiles, made new friends, and soon was busily engaged in editorial and cultural activities, serving as unofficial adviser, for instance, in the founding of the excellent literary magazine *Asomante*. In short, he could live again in an atmosphere similar to that of pre-Civil War Spain.

Todo más claro (*All Things Made Clearer*), 1949, on the other hand, is closely associated with Salinas' residence on the U.S. mainland, and particularly with urban life in the megalopolis of the upper eastern seaboard. At the request of his Argentine editor, Salinas wrote a short preface for this book, in which he partially clarifies its narrative context. This poetry was written in the United States between 1937 and 1947. Salinas points out the paradox involved in the choice of a title which hardly seems appropriate for a book speaking mainly of the anguish of man in modern times. He states his intention of presenting the vision of a science-fiction mechanistic world surpassing even the chaotic nightmares painted by Hieronymus Bosch or Goya. He adds that this nightmare has been created by modern science which, in the name of progress, is preparing man's total destruction, both spiritually and literally, in warfare.

Having raised the question of the curious title, Salinas gives an evasive aesthetic reason for his choice. Clearly, a promise of some form of salvation is implied in the title, and Salinas' drawing attention to it is his warning to the reader that he should not interpret this book as a totally despairing view of the future. The clue to the title's choice lies in the book's structure, as we shall see. Taken out of context, several poems might be interpreted as totally defeatist. Considering the book as a whole, however, we shall see that its message is, conditionally, one of hope; substantially the same message as that expressed in *The Contemplated Sea*.

The same can be said for the posthumous *Confianza* (*Confidence*), written between 1942 and 1944 and published posthumously (1955). In this last book, it is impossible to rely on structure for the corroboration of theme, since Salinas himself did not arrange the poems in their final order. The text, as it appears in the first edition, was compiled by Juan Marichal, with the advice of Salinas' lifelong friend, Jorge Guillén. The title was borrowed from the last poem which seems to epitomize the mood of the book and could be interpreted as Salinas' ultimate profession of faith.

From the dates given above, it is apparent that the three books overlap chronologically. It is entirely possible that Salinas wrote poems included later in *All Things Made Clearer* at approximately the same time that he was writing others destined to find their place in *Confidence* or *The Contemplated Sea*. This is all the more reason to see all this poetry as intimately related.

III The Contemplated Sea: *A Profession of Faith*

The Contemplated Sea is made up of an initial poem entitled "Tema," followed by fourteen titled "Variations." Six poems are written in otosyllabic verses (interspersed with occasional verses of from four to five syllables), and two (Variations VII and XIV) in hendecasyllables. Alternating with this series, we find a second group of six poems written in couplets of one hendecasyllable with a seven-syllable *enjambement* (in Variation IX, the combination is 8-6). The entire book is a sustained dialogue of the poet with the sea, object of this contemplation. Gustavo Correa has noted that the poem operates on four levels. The first is simply the description and praise of the beauty of nature—seascape, sky, clouds, beaches, and islets—all joined in cosmic harmony in the island paradise of Puerto Rico.[6] This reality immediately perceived, as always with Salinas, is then given poetic meaning, and the process of recreation from a real to a poetically meaningful world—the poetic process as theme—is the second level of meaning. The third and fourth levels are intimately related on metaphyiscal and symbolic planes equivalent to the second and third stages of spiritual perfection according to Teilhard de Chardin's theories. The poet finds personal justification and fulfillment in a spiritual communion with a Being greater than himself.

As in *Love's Reason*, the sea emerges as the symbol of an essential reality, eternal, immutable and complete in itself, yet constantly recreating itself in an endless dynamic cycle. Correa also notes that the dominant motif in the entire poem is the image of the sea as an orchard or as a garden in spring, fecundated by light, and giving forth a daily harvest of flowers and fruit. In short, the motif of the sea as Edenic Paradise, already introduced in *Love's Reason*, is completed in this poem.

Andrew Debicki also discovered that the book possesses a dynamic narrative structure through which a reversal of roles in the dialogue between poet and sea becomes evident,[7] this time, in the inverse order from that perceived in *The Voice Owed to You*. In the "Tema" and first four variations, the protagonist is clearly the poet in his role of interpreter and transformer of reality. The artist is very much imbued with his personal role in the conquest of a passive element in need of him to be revealed in all its meaning:

¡Sí tú has sido para mí, (Yes! You have [truly] been for me,

desde el día from the day on which
que mis ojos te estrenaron, my eyes first brought out [your beauty]

el contemplado, el constante the contemplated one, the constant

Contemplado! ("Tema," p. 551) Contemplated One!)

Si te nombro, soy tu amo (If I call your name, I own you
de un segundo. ¡Qué milagro! for one instant. What a miracle!)
("Variation III," p. 556)

Beginning with "Variation V," however, the roles are reversed. The constancy of the sea's beauty provides for the poet not a changing reality always in need of definition, but one which demands contemplation in depth; a material world already reduced to essential qualities. The poet now takes on a more passive role, and the sea becomes a guide which he follows blindly. Clarity, far from being an element which the poet adds to reality, is now an essential attribute of the sea itself:

Tú, Lazarillo de ojos (You, O blindman's guide of the eyes,

llévate a estos míos; guíalos, show them the path and lead them,

. . . .

A tu resplandor me entrego, I am surrendering to your radiance

igual que el ciego a la mano, as a blindman to a [guiding] hand

. . . .

Con mi vista, que te mira, With my sight, as I look at you,
poco te doy, mucho gano. I give so little, gain so much.
Sale de mis ojos, pobre, In poverty, it leaves my eyes,
se me marcha por tus campos, it moves forward across your fields

coge azules, brillos, olas, picks blues [like flowers], speckles, waves

alegrías, and gaieties,
las dádivas de tu espacio. the rich bequest of your expanse.
Cuando vuelve, vuelve toda And in returning, it comes back
encendida de regalos. resplendently alit with gifts.

. . . .

¡De lo claro que lo enseñas A miracle, and yet, so clear,
qué sencillo es el milagro! it seems simplicity itself.
Si bien se guarda en los ojos, If we can hold it in our eyes,
nunca pasa, lo pasado. the past will never fade away.) *
(pp. 559-60)

It is clear that the newly discovered reality of the sea is different from any other previously encountered by the poet. Before, his role had been to capture in brief flashes of intuition the essential beauty of a moment, and to hope to recreate a parallel experience in others by means of a poem. It was the poet's role to give reality an element of performance for the benefit of others. But the new reality perceived in the sea already possesses permanence. Reality, creator, and poetic creation, are all together symbolically personified by the sea. In "Variation VI," the sea performs the function which, previously, the poet had assigned to himself:

> *En el confín te nace de tus aires*
> *un pensamiento vago.*

. . . .

Ya frentes más serenas—ondas—onda,
a onda, le van pensando.

. . . .

el pensamiento aquel nacido oscuro,
lo pone todo en claro. (pp. 562-63)

(Within your realm, engendered by your winds
a nascent thought emerges.

. . . .

Already calmer brows—of the waves—from wave
to wave, give it meaning.

. . . .

this thought born hesitant and obscure
now colors everything with brightness.)

"Variation VIII" is entitled "Renacimiento de Venus" ("Re-
birth of Venus"). The Venus who is reborn from the sea is
not a woman but Life, presenting itself in an absolute present
always within reach. Critics have noted that in this poem Salinas
comes closer than ever to the poetry of Guillén's *Cántico,* both in
spirit and in style.[8] Like Guillén, Salinas gives us a static vision
of a world perfect in itself, independently of any beholder:

Está el día en el fiel. La luz, la sombra
ni más ni menos pesan.

. . . .

El presente, que tanto se ha negado,
hoy, aquí, ya se entrega.

. . . .

Radiante mediodía. En él, el alma
se reconoce: esencia. (pp. 567-68)

(The day has reached its equilibrium. Light and shadow
bear down with equal evidence.

. . . .

Pure present for so long elusive
here, today, surrenders itself.

. . . .

Radiant noon in which the soul
is mirrored in its own essence.)

In "Variation VI," the sea performs the function which, pre-
explained. Happiness in a perfect present is compared to that

brought about in any perfect love relationship. But this new Love Goddess is not content with embracing only one lover. The poet is conscious of his common place among myriads of lovers, past, present, and future:

[. . .] belleza a nadie negada,	(a beauty denied to no one,
a nadie ofrecida.	directed to no single man.
No quiere la luz por dueña	Light will not owe allegiance
ninguna pupila;	to any eyes;
el sol nace para todos,	the sun is born for everyone
y en nadie termina.	and surrenders to no one.
Y esa amante misteriosa,	And this mysterious lover
fugaz, entrevista,	fugitive and caught in a glimpse
. . . .	. . . .
no es nunca amante, es la amada	is never a lover, but the total
total. Es la vida. (p. 571)	loved One. Life itself.)

"Variations X" and "XI" are homages to the sea as the supreme poet, creator of fables and myths, and always successful in its endless task of recreating beauty. The sea thus becomes a symbol of the repository of culture which Salinas sees as engaged in a continuous self-perfective development. Again, we are struck with the similarity of Salinas' ideas with theological thought. For Teilhard de Chardin, God is the ultimate goal and purpose of a spiritual evolutionary process. Salinas does not mention God, but he does seem to envision an Edenic existence in which humanity will ultimately find its permanent reward. Such a promise is held in the final verses of "Variation XI":

¡El acierto! ¿Vendrá? ¡Si!	(Victory! Will it come? It will!
. . . .	. . . .
Vendrá cuando al universo	It will come when the universe
se le aclare la razón	gains awareness of the ultimate
final de tu movimiento	purpose in your movement:
no moverse, mediodía.	to be motionless at full noon.
. . . .	. . . .
La plena consumación	In fullest consummation
—al amor, igual, igual—	—toward love, constant, constant—
de tanto ardor en sosiego.	of such burning and tranquil de-
	sire.)

(pp. 578-79)

"Variation XII," "Civitas Dei" ("The City of God"), is a
long poem in three parts. It is important in that it provides
a link with Salinas' following book, *All Things Made Clearer*.
The poet establishes a contrast between the City of God, the
perfect essential reality embodied in the sea, and the contingent daily reality to which he must now return. For modern
man, it is a pragmatic world, intent only on material gain, the
slave of time and of a mechanized existence, a world where
everything is gauged in terms of exact quantities and numbers:

> Aquel aire infinito lo han contado;
>   números se respiran.
> El tiempo ya no es tiempo, el tiempo es oro,
>   florecen compañías
> para vender a plazos los veranos,
>   las horas y los días.
> Luchan las cantidades con los pájaros,
>   los nombres con las cifras: [. . .] (pp. 581-82)

> (They have measured this infinite air:
>   we're breathing numbers.
> Time is no longer time, time is gold,
>   companies flourish
> by selling summers, hours and days
>   on time payment.
> Quantities are struggling with birds
>   and names with numbers . . .)

The reality of a modern dehumanized world is thus a superficial reality: *[. . .] un edén de cartón piedra* (a pasteboard
Eden) compared to the eternal beauty of nature. The danger
lies in that men have become captives of this technical illusion.
Science and technology are being used to stifle life and poetry.
As we shall see in the discussion of *All Things Made Clearer*,
this implied message is substantially the same as that presented
by Lorca in *Poet in New York*. Only a few poets are left to
point the way to salvation, and this is their new assigned
mission. In "Civitas Dei" the symbol of innocent man, desperately striving to escape the tyranny of modern times, is Charlie
Chaplin.

The last two variations restate the general theme of the

poem and reaffirm the poet's new position in the final stage of
spiritual maturity:

> *Poseído voluntario*
> *de esta fuerza que me invade,*
> *mayor soy, porque me siento*
> *yo mismo, y enajenado.* ("Variation XIII," p. 587)

> (Possessed voluntarily
> by this [great] strength which invades me
> I am larger [than life-size], feeling
> that I'm myself, while transcending my own bounds.)

The message of *The Contemplated Sea* can be summarized as
follows: The sea is a symbol for life itself, both the permanent
human feelings and the beauties of nature as contemplated by
generations since the creation of man.

It is enough for Salinas to know that even though he must
die one day, the beauty he perceived in the sea is permanent.
It is no longer reality which is illusory, but each viewer whose
life time destroys. Salinas' previous conflicts are resolved when
he ceases to attach value to the realization of his individual
self (important only in so far as he is able to assimilate and
communicate beauty to others). The poet is only one link in
the chain; the chain is the important thing. Salinas thus has
traded individual happiness for a greater happiness of sharing
and feeling a common bond with all humanity. *The Contemplated Sea* ends on the following Profession of Faith:

> *Que por mis ojos, suyos, miren ellos*
> *y todos mis hermanos anteriores,*
> *sepultos por los siglos*
> *ciegos de muerte: vista les devuelvo.*
> . . . .
> *Y de tanto mirarte, nos salvemos.* ("Variation XIV," p. 589)

> (Let my eyes be theirs, serving as their guide
> and that of all my former brothers
> buried across the centuries
> blinded by death: I give them new sight.
> . . . .
> And in your contemplation let us find our salvation.)

IV   All Things Made Clearer: *The Descent into Hell*

The Contemplated Sea expresses with the greatest clarity
Salinas' new philosophy of life, and in this respect is probably
his most significant book. Yet, it never quite attains the lyrical
level of the love cycle or the intensity of feeling of *All Things
Made Clearer*, which is perhaps the book with which the contemporary reader can best identify. No one can fail to empa-
thize with the poet's desperate struggle to preserve his faith in
the future of humanity while at the same time facing squarely
the inherent dangers of its destruction through the misuse of
technology.

By the time *All Things Made Clearer* was completed, in 1947,
Salinas had been the recent witness to nine consecutive years
of armed conflict. Modern warfare seemed to him the one real
threat to culture, and he became obsessed with the fear of
total destruction. His long poem "Cero" ("Zero"), first published
individually in a Spanish-English bilingual edition,[9] then added
as the last poem of *All Things Made Clearer* (1949), was
written in 1944 and has seemed to many an uncanny prophecy
of the Hiroshima holocaust which was to take place only a few
months later. The protest against war is also a dominant theme
of Salinas' novel, *La bomba increíble* (*The Incredible Bomb*),
which I shall discuss in the next chapter.

The majority of critics, mostly on the basis of isolated poems,
have insisted on the pessimistic aspect of *All Things Made
Clearer*. It is true that Salinas resolutely rejects the materialistic
values of modern society. But he also offers an alternative to
these values which he exposes as being only deceitful illusions.
Once again he expresses a Proustian faith in poetry and in art's
ability to preserve and transmit the more permanent values
of life and culture. The poet's ethical mission is reiterated in the
first part of the book, and it is to this ethical mission that the
general title of the volume refers. Although the full title is *All
Things Made Clearer, and Other Poems*, it is not a random
collection, but like all of Salinas' mature works, possesses a
narrative structure which requires all the poems to be read in
sequence and in context to be properly understood.

The collection is made up of thirteen titled poems, some quite

long and further divided into sections indicated by subtitles or
Roman numerals. The first poem, subtitled "Camino del poema"
("Toward the Poem"). is a restatement of earlier ideas on the
development of the poetic process from initial perception to the
legacy of the poem. Subtitles give a clue to the symbolic value
of each of its four divisions. In Division I, "Las cosas"
("Things"), p. 599, repeats the assertion that material things
should be looked at as only "presages" of a deeper *trasrrealidad*
Division II, "En ansias inflamada" ("Burning with longings"),
p. 601, is an obvious reference to the Mystics' "dark night of the
soul" the inner contemplation in which the poet proceeds from
perception to vision. Division III, "Verbo" ("The Word"), p.
603, is the slow translation of this vision into words, and Division
IV, *"El poema"* ("The Poem"), p. 607, refers to the final creation
to be handed down to future generations. The theme of this
general introduction is thus that of poetry as key to immortality.
The second poem, "El inocente" ("The Innocent Ones"), p. 611,
opposes the dreaming *yo* of the poet inventor of "fables," to
the pragmatic *yo* forced to live amidst daily deceptions. These
antagonistic aspects of the poet's personality face each other
in subsequent poems which picture first a descent into Hell,
and then the poet's subsequent rescue. While the anguished
yo representing modern man at first almost succumbs to feelings of alienation and despair, the dreaming *yo*, like a guardian
angel, will slowly point the way to salvation. The function of
this *inocente* is made explicit at the end of the second poem:

> *Vislumbro salvación: es el respeto*
> *al inocente mío, al trapecista;*
> *guardar, guardar, acordes, la distancia*
> *que al hombre le distingue de su sueño.*
> *El hombre, mientras viva.* (pp. 616-17)

> (I sense a salvation in the respect
> for my innocent self, on his flying trapeze;
> in preserving and maintaining carefully, the distance
> which distinguishes man from his dream.
> While man still lives.)

The stage is thus set for a bitter denunciation of modern life.
Part I begins in the form of a walk through a modern cos-

mopolis later clearly identified as New York. It opens with the book's most anguished poems, reminiscent both in feeling and in imagery of Lorca's *Poet in New York*. The vision is that of a totally automated society, in which men and machines move at a frenetic pace. This vision is adequately symbolized in the third poem, "Hombre en la orilla" ("Man Standing on the Shore"), by the flow of traffic in a Manhattan street. Lorca, for whom as for Salinas water had always been a symbol of life, described New York crowds as a sterile stream of dry feet: *agua harapienta de los pies secos*.[10] Salinas' protagonist pictures himself as a terrified human form about to be engulfed by a torrent of speeding cars, the very opposite of the river-symbol of earlier poems: *Este río no es aquel:/ corriente, a secas./ Alveo que ignora el agua* (This river is not that former [stream]:/ it's just a current./ A riverbed ignorant of water).

With each passing car, an insight into the preoccupations of its driver reveals a total enslavement to economic gain, relieved only briefly in the pursuit of escapist pleasures. Mrs. Dorothy Morrison, 37, in a race with her watch speeds on to keep an appointment at the beauty parlor which will restore the appearance of her lost youth. An actor thinks only of his next film and his ever increasing earnings, and Jim, the adolescent student, though still responding confusedly to the beauties of nature, is already engulfed in the vertiginous pursuit of his career.

In Part II of the same poem, the narrator, standing on the edge of the false riverbank, becomes aware of the full implication of this mad race at full speed toward death. In him, man's millenial fear of the void is joined with a more modern anguish before imminent destruction:

Y en el mundo sólo él,	(And in the world, only he,
este hombre que tiembla,	this man [who stands there] trembling
siente por la vez primera	experiences for the first time,
junto al terror más antiguo,	along with that most ancient terror,
el pánico de las selvas,	that [primitive] fear of the jungle,
y al espanto del milenio,	and the millenary anguish,
y al horror frío que asciende	and the aseptic horror rising

del microscopio y su hallazgo,	from the microscope and its findings,
más terror, otro terror,	more fear, another terror;
esta pavidez, tan nueva	this strange new-born panic
que le tiene aquí, clavado	which keeps him standing here, fastened
en el borde	to the edge
de ella, la terrible acera. (p. 626)	of its shore, that menacing sidewalk.)

What he now feels is not so much an existential revulsion before an absurd or gratuitous life, but the awareness that centuries of progress are being negated in this insane renunciation of all spiritual pursuit. It is as if all the dreams and desires of the past are to be sacrificed. This threat awakens in modern man a feeling of a responsibility which goes far beyond the salvation of his own self:

Y en su puente el genovés	(And the Genoese upon his bridge,
y en Koenigsberga el filósofo,	and in Koenigsberg, the philosopher,
¿al final, qué les espera:	What will await them in the end,
un mar vacío, o un mundo,	a vacant sea, or a [meaningful] world,
conocer, no conocer?	knowing, or not knowing?
. . . .	. . . .
A muchos les ha tocado	For many the bell has tolled
esta hora atroz	the fearful eleventh-hour
la del hombre de la orilla:	that faces man standing on the shore
verse enfrente de la O. (p. 628)	[alone], face to face with the O.)

In a last moment of utter panic, modern man is faced with the decision of letting himself be engulfed by the invading torrent of wheels, or, by crossing the lethal river, of finding means to transcend its dangers.

Salinas pictures this present-day Everyman as already so spiritually numb as to be unable to distinguish the paths which could lead to his salvation from those which will decree his certain death. His indecision is symbolized by his pause before a traffic light, alternating between green and red flashes:

El hombre sigue en la orilla,	(As man remains upon the shore
Ve destellos. También dos.	He sees [bright] beams. Also two
Alternativos relumbres,	alternating flashes,
pero ¿claridades? No [. . .]	but clarifications? Hardly . . .
. . . .	. . . .
¡Gravísima indecisión	A most serious indecision
verdi-rojo, muerte-vida!	between green and red, life and
	death!
Las ruedas perdonan todo	The wheels might forgive every-
	thing
menos el último error.	except that last miscalculation.)

(pp. 632-33)

The modern dilemma having been clearly defined in these verses, the scene shifts to the more peaceful visions conjured up by the dreaming "I." In the city, churches and museums are islands of peace. The fourth poem, "Santo de palo" ("Wooden Saint"), shows the protagonist in contemplation of the medieval wooden statue of a saint. The mortal being of a distant generation has been immortalized into a work of art. The artist's "soul," transcending the matter of this primitive wood carving, still lives in unison with those who see his work across the centuries.

In Number V, "Pasajero en museo" ("Passenger in a Museum"), the poet is aware of his condition as a "passenger of life" facing immortal beings represented in great paintings:

> *Con esos ojos de ultravida, vivos,*
> *a mí, a mí me miráis, desvanecido*
> *mortal, que vine a veros,*
> *tan cegado de historias y catálogos*
> *que os daba por muertos.*
> . . . .
> *[. . .] echando voy mi vida sucesiva*
> *de quehacer en quehacer, de gesto en gesto*
> *sobre el espacio blanco de los días,*
> *pobre imagen de cine*
> *huyendo de haz en haz, sin encontrarse.*
> . . . .
> *Y aquí estoy, frente a otras: criaturas*
> *a tiempo, para siempre, detenidas*
> *en sólo una actividad, la que eterniza.*
> . . . .

Vuestra vida es de cima, calma augusta. (pp. 643-46)

. . . .

(With your gaze from beyond the tomb, so alive,
you look at me, at me, the insignificant
mortal who came to see you
so blind with learned data and catalogues
that I had thought of you as dead.

. . . .

. . . I am casting my transitory life
from chore to chore and from gesture to gesture
on the blank space of each successive day;
a pitiful image on a screen,
fleeing from spotlight to spotlight without finding itself.

. . . .

And now I stand before these other beings
who reached their goal, forever frozen
within one sole gesture; that which immortalized [them].

. . . .

Your lives, immobilized at their peak, in august calm.)

But the poet understands that if these now transcendent beings
have earned immortality, it was at the cost of severing all bonds
with what once constituted their existence as individuals of
flesh and blood:

> *Sí vuestra salvación fue la renuncia*
> *a lo que hay a este lado de los marcos;*
> *vivir, seguir, querer seguir viviendo.* (p. 647)

> (Truly, you were saved by your renunciation
> of what faces you outside your picture frames;
> a life that goes on; the wish to go on living.)

The implied message is that to be saved is to renounce volun-
tarily any values fatally anchored in matter and in passing life.
As the protagonist leaves the museum, he faces a beautiful sun-
set bathing the geometric forms of the city in soft redeeming
light. But this celestial beauty too is ephemeral, conditioned by
the movements of day and night: . . . *ella, hermana inmensa/*
igual que yo declina eternidades (She, my spacious sister/ like
me declines to live eternally), p. 648. Clearly, there can be no

salvation merely in the passing enjoyment of life. The poet must somehow transcend his earthly condition, losing all hope for a permanent individual happiness, but exchanging it for a greater collective one.

The next poem, "La vocación" ("The Vocation"), is in praise of poetic inspiration which will enable the poet to give eternity to perceived moments in poems as equally lasting as the paintings he has just seen in the museum. His first immortality will be gained by the poetic function of giving an eternal soul to matter. But immortality as mere literary fame would be a pale consolation. The poet's work must be a work of love, and his supreme justification that of sharing his personal feelings with the community of men. "Nocturno de los avisos" ("Nocturne of the Signs") is the poet's final consideration, and rejection, of the values of modern civilization, ending with his opting for a more harmonious reality. It is one of the book's most beautiful poems, and, as it represents a good thematic synthesis of the entire book, I will later return to it for a detailed analysis.

"Angel extraviado" ("Lost Angel") relates the final battle between the two aspects of the poet's divided self: modern man against the Angel of Hope who has come to his rescue. The battle ends in the acceptance of the supreme sacrifice, that of renouncing a mortal body which cannot be prized too highly, since it finds no justification in itself. The poet will find salvation in putting his immortal poetic soul at the service of others, in a supreme act of solidarity and love:

¡Victoria! No la mía,
yo pobre, yo sin armas.

(A victory! [But] not my own—
I [am] weak, I [stand] without
    weapons.

El triunfo en mí, feliz,
de las alas del mundo.

Within me, the happy triumph
of the wings of the world.

. . . .

Yo soy sólo las manos
que tiende aquél que quiere
al otro, en su flaqueza.
Las manos del que ama
con ansia vividora
se terminan en ángeles.
                    (pp. 665-67)

I am only the hands
of him who, loving another,
reaches out, sensing his weakness.
A man's hands if he truly loves
with life-giving earnestness
have the destiny of the angels.)

"Lost Angel" was the prelude to the third "act" of *All Things Made Clearer*; "Entretiempo romántico ("Romantic Interlude"),[11] dedicated to a definition of love. Its first poem, *"Adiós con variaciones"* ("A Good-Bye with Variations"), p. 671, is a condemnation of the Romantic adventure, every man's dream, forever pursued, of finding the perfect love relationship with the ideal woman. The entire poem is a parody of a sentimentalized romantic setting, in which two lovers embrace each other in a slow waltz. A waltz which for one moment makes them believe in the eternity of their love:

> *Nos quedaremos solos,*
> *en este gran salón, color de almendra,*
> *dando vueltas y vueltas*
> *como un mundo los dos, un mundo solo*
> *sobre un amor girando*
> *conforme aquella ley que descubrimos*
> *una tarde de estío en dos miradas.* (pp. 673-74)

> (Alone we shall remain,
> in this immense almond-colored ballroom,
> whirling, endlessly whirling,
> the two of us sharing one world, a private world
> spinning upon one [mutual] love
> by virtue of the law which we discovered
> on a summer evening, in our mutual gaze.)

The final verses of this passage echo some of the neo-Romantic poems of Alberti or Aleixandre.[12] We remember that their attitude in contemplating the shattered love-ideal had ended in rebellion. But in the present poem, there is no regret. After the experience of *The Voice Owed to You*, the poet is able to reject any solution based on an individual love affair which, however beautiful and even lasting until death, would still be exposed as a transitory illusion:

> *[............] el amor*
> *sólo sabe la altura a que vivía*
> *cuando la ha de bajar, y cuando cuenta*
> *cada peldaño que llevaba el gozo*
> *con cifras de cristal*

que tibiamente caen por las mejillas.

....

Y al ver cómo tus ojos se cerraban
comprendí lo inminente:
que el mar iba a volver por lo que es suyo. (pp. 674–75)

....

(. . . . . love
only [really] knows what lofty heights it reached
when forced to abandon them, only to count
every step which led to [supreme] happiness
with numbers made of crystals
softly rolling down [the two lover's] cheeks

....

And as I saw your eyelids [slowly] closing
I sensed the imminent return
of the sea, come to reclaim its own possession.)

The poem does not end in total despair, since the last verse
quoted reminds us that the lovers will not die forever but be
reinstated in the universal "sea of love" which Salinas had described in *Love's Reason*.

In the light of the previous poem, Salinas can describe the
woman's body as an empty myth in "El cuerpo fabuloso" ("The
Fabulous Body"), p. 676. He will only remember the lover's
essence, the "Thou" which made him begin the process of
decentralization of the self, in the second phase of spiritual
evolution.

"Error de cálculo" ("Error in Calculation"), p. 680, is a satire
of a de-romanticized love affair in modern times. Contemporary
lovers have shunned the whole Romantic apparatus and ideals.
Love is reduced to sensual attraction, emerging from a casual
encounter in a fashionable bar. It begins with a flirtatious
"battle of the sexes." These lovers deal with the planned adventure with simulated indifference, and their love is described
almost as a business transaction, weighed in terms of cold
numbers:

¡Qué solos, y qué cerca, entre la gente!
Perfecta intimidad, exenta de romanzas
de cisnes e ilusiones,
sin más paisaje al fondo

que el arco iris de las botellas de licores
y la lluvia menuda
de frases ingeniosas—salida de teatro—
con que corbatas blancas y descotes, de once a doce,
asesinan despacio un día más.
. . . .

Hablar de nuestras almas, de su gran agonía,
como se habla de un negocio,
con las inteligencias afiladas,
huyendo de la selva virgen donde vivimos
en busca de ese sólido asfalto de los cálculos,
de las cifras exactas, inventores
de una aritmética de almas que nos salve
de todo error futuro [. . . . .] (pp. 680-81)

(How alone [we are] and yet how near among
      the crowds!
a perfect intimacy devoid of love ballads,
of swans, and of illusions,
with no scenery before us
except the rainbow of the brandy bottles,
and the constant drizzle
—after the theater—of witty repartee
with which white ties and low-cut gowns, in the
      late midnight hour,
slowly bring a day to its final death.
. . . .

To speak of our [secret] souls, of their deep suffering
as one might speak of business
with our intelligence sharpened to a fine edge,
abandoning the virgin forests in which we dwelt
in search of the solid asphalt of computations,
of precise numbers, the inventors
of an arithmetic for the soul, which might save us
from all future miscalculations . . . .)

The lovers soon realize the futility of the effort to "calculate"
the perfect combination for a lasting adventure: an illusion
as great as the romantic make-believe which they had scorned.
But suddenly, in a flash of inspiration, the protagonist begins
to see the couples seated around him in another light. They
assume the disguise and appearance of great lovers of the past:

De una mesa de al lado se levanta
una pareja; son Venus y Apolo
con disfraz de Abelardo y Eloísa
. . . .
Pasan junto a un espejo y en el mundo
se ven dos más, dos más, dos más. De pronto
se me figura, todo alucinado,
que podríamos ser una pareja
tú y yo, si tú y si yo . . . Voy recordando
. . . .
que allá, en el paraíso,
hubo otros dos, primeros, que empezamos
separados o juntos, tú y yo, todos,
por ser una pareja; [. . . . .] (p. 683)

(From a neighboring table a couple
rises; it is Venus and Apollo
disguised as Abelard and Heloise.
. . . .
They stop before a mirror and the world reflects
another pair, another and another. Suddenly
transfigured, I dare imagine
that we could be one more [immortal] pair
you and I, yes, if you and I only could . . . and
   I remember
. . . .
that long ago in paradise
other lovers, the first ones, existed. That we began
separately or jointly, you and I,
because we were a pair, ...)

The poet sees the possibility of rejoining these eternal lovers, of gaining immortality by being reincarnations of their love. If their own individual love is great enough, they will meet death with the certainty of transcending their mortal condition by becoming perfect links in the eternal chain of human love.

This is the essential message of *All Things Made Clearer*, an optimistic one, though born of despair and ending in an attitude perilously close to escape from reality, as well as rebellion against the cold reality of modern times. In this book there is less emphasis than in any other book on acceptance and enjoyment of everyday life. But this is not surprising in the face of the horrors

which for Salinas, as well as Lorca in *Poet in New York,* had
already made the poetic transformation of reality a near impossibility. Such an extreme position was at any rate only
temporary (and we must not forget that at the same time Salinas
was writing poems expressing a different view).

Two remaining poems are but weak complements of this
section dedicated to the definition of love. "Lo inútil" ("Useless
Things") states a vague yearning for everything that is not
measurable and pragmatic, and concludes that: *el sino de la
vida es lo incompleto* (the destiny of life is incompleteness), an
echo of Salinas' earlier allegiance to "steadfast chance." "Contra
esta primavera" ("Against the Spring"), p. 695, is a rejection of
every year's and every lover's spring, substituting a spring which
is a state of mind, outside temporal circumstances:

> [. . .] *amar, estar amando*
> *cuando los otros dicen*
> *mirándose las fechas*
> *"Espera, aun no se puede,*
> *el amor, ahora, duerme."*
> *Canta su savia altísima*
> *en una noche fría*
> *el impulso del amor.*
> . . . .
> *Canta el don de alegrarse sin modelo*
> *inventor de su métrica.* (p. 698)

> (. . . to be under the spell of love
> when everyone else is saying
> with an eye to the calendar
> "Wait a little, [it isn't time,]
> you can't love yet: love's still asleep."
> The resonant sap of his song
> rings aloud in the chill of the night.
> It sings of the impulse of love.
> . . . .
> It sings of the gift of rejoicing without a precedent
> the inventor of its own poetry.)*

The final act of *All Things Made Clearer* contains the poet's
protest against war. In its original plan, "El viento y la guerra"

("Wind and War"), p. 703, was to end the volume. It is not an
entirely convincing poem, and stylistically it reminds one of
Salinas' first period. The subject of war is treated allegorically,
as the word *guerra*, written on a blank sheet of paper, is seen
as the abstract impediment to poetry, as well as the essence of
a dehumanizing civilization. It is, however, finally erased by
passing winds, symbolizing the forces of nature. In this poem,
Salinas seems still rather optimistic about humanity's ability to
cope with the madness of war.

"Cero" ("Zero"), p. 709, on the other hand, is a long poem
divided into five parts, which describes in gripping terms the
destruction of a city by bombing. In Part I, the bomb is dropped
from the sky by an indifferent aviator who, not seeing the masses
of humanity he is about to destroy, cannot partake in any feelings toward them. He is the victim of machines, himself a pro-
grammed robot carrying out unerringly the work of destruction
dictated by precise instruments which timed a tragedy to the
exact second. A screen of white fluffy clouds rising from the
earth as the bomb explodes actually adds a note of beauty to
the scene, convincing the bomber of the inoffensiveness of
his mission.

Parts II and III describe the happiness that could have been
had the world been left to fulfill its destiny. Again, we see
Salinas' visions of reality in cumulative perfection, and in
constant evolution toward a greater sum of Life and beauty:

> [. . . . .] *Cuando rueda*
> *el mundo, tesorero, va sumando*
> *—en cada vuelta gana una, hermosura*
> *a belleza de ayer, belleza inédita.*
> *Sobre sus hombros gráciles las horas*
> *dádivas imprevistas acarrean.*
> *¿Vida? Invención, hallazgo, lo que es*
> *hoy a las cuatro, y a las tres no era.* (p. 715)

> (. . . . . The revolving world,
> like a treasure keeper, adds on new riches
> —with every turn, it finds new loveliness
> in yesterday's beauty, an unrecorded splendor.
> The small and slender backs of every hour

are laden with never envisioned presents.
Be it life, a creation, or a discovery, something
today, at four o'clock, which at three was lacking.) *

But the bomb frustrates the promise of this future perfection.
Parts IV and V show the full brutality of war and in the annihilation of accumulated centuries of culture, the destruction
of the chain:

> ¡Y todos, ahora, todos,
> qué naufragio total, en este escombro!
> No tibios, no despedazados miembros
> me piden compasión, desde la ruina:
> de carne antigua voz antigua, oigo.
> . . . .
> No piso la materia; en su pedriza
> piso el mayor dolor, tiempo deshecho.
> . . . .
> Lo que era suma en un instante es polvo.
> ¡Qué derroche de siglos, un momento!
> . . . .
> Se abre por fin la tumba a que escaparon;
> les llega aquí la muerte de que huyeron.
> Ya encontré mi cadáver, el que lloro.
> Cadáver de los muertos que vivían
> salvados de sus cuerpos pasajeros.
> Un gran silencio en el vacío oscuro,
> un gran polvo de obras, triste incienso,
> canto infinito, funeral sin nadie. (pp. 720-22)

(And all of them, now, all of them,
behold their total shipwreck in this pile of rubble!
No, it is not the still warm and shattered limbs
which now, from the wreckage, are pleading for mercy:
from a [more] ancient flesh I hear an ancient voice.
. . . .
I do not tread on matter, among these stones
I stand on the greater sorrow of Time destroyed.
. . . .
What was once a sum, in one instant is dust.
What extravagant waste of centuries, in one moment!
. . . .

At last, the grave from which they escaped is opened.
Here this death which they had avoided reaches them.
At last I have found the corpse which I mourn.
The remains of all the dead, who lived on,
once preserved, outside their transitory bodies.
A vast silence which fills the darkest void,
a great dusty wreckage, a mock tribute,
an infinite elegy, a funeral with no one present.)

Faced with the possibility of total destruction, and the failure of his spiritual system, the attitude of Salinas could only be that of the rebel. We are reminded of Goya's reaction before the disasters of war, and of the change that took place in the mind of this disciple of the Age of Reason, great believer in progress, when he attempted to translate the bestiality of men at war. The final verses of Salinas' poem are inspired perhaps by that baffling painting, from Goya's black period, "Dog Buried in Sand," in which the head of a dog pathetically emerges from the gray matter about to engulf it:

Pero aúlla un perro, un infinito perro
—inmenso aullar nocturno ¿desde dónde?—
voz clamante entre minas por su dueño. (p. 722)

(But somewhere, a dog howls, an infinite dog
—this loud nocturnal howl, where does it come from?—
a voice from within the earth is calling for its owner.)

The change in the level of language between the poetry of the Love Cycle and that of *The Contemplated Sea,* on the one hand, and that of *All Things Made Clearer* on the other, should be apparent to any reader even without much analysis. In *The Voice Owed to You* and *Love's Reason,* we were accustomed to an elegant, at times "precious," style, and to the harmonious cadences inspired in the Renaissance models of Garcilaso and Fray Luis. Similarly, the style of *The Contemplated Sea* has been compared with that of the Golden Age mystic, San Juan de la Cruz. In all three books, Salinas' verses seek to appease and to reflect the order and beauty of an harmonious vision.

In *All Things Made Clearer*, particularly in the poems which are an indictment of modern life, Salinas often attempts to shock his reader. His use of parody and satire, for instance, has already been pointed out in the two poems quoted from "Romantic Interlude." In this book, he generally speaks in plain everyday language, and through symbolic levels of meaning less remote and esoteric than in previous books. The immediate relationship between a world of real, clearly identifiable objects, and their poetic equivalents, is also much more apparent than before.

Yet, Salinas' language is never commonplace. It remains "learned," chiefly through the use of many mythological or cultural-literary allusions (and an occasional conceptual metaphor) which at first might seem out of place in a description of contemporary reality. Taking one poem, "Nocturno de los avisos" ("Nocturne of the Signs") as an example, we shall see that this paradoxical mixture has its purpose. In dealing with a dehumanized and mechanical world, it represents Salinas' attempt at ironic idealization, making even more obvious the total lack of inherent beauty in the reality he describes. In spite of its length, and because I consider it perhaps Salinas' most perfect single poem, I shall quote the poem in full:

"Nocturno de los avisos"	"Nocturne of the Signs"
¿Quién va a dudar de ti, la rectilínea, que atraviesa el mundo tan derecha	(Who would doubt you, the rectilinear one, who follows its course through the world as directly
como el asceta, entre las tentaciones?	as the ascetic, among temptations?
Todos acatan, hasta el más rebelde, tus rigurosas normas paralelas:	Everyone holds in awe, even the most rebellious, your rigorous parallel patterns:
aceras, el arroyo, los rieles del tranvía, tus orillas, altísimos ribazos	sidewalks, the stream, the streetcar rails, your shores, steep embankments
sembrados de ventanas, hierba espesa, que a la noche rebrilla	sown with windows, thick-grown grass that glitters in the night

10

con gotas de eléctrico rocío.
Infinita a los ojos
y toda numerada, a cada paso

un algo nos revelas
de dos en dos, muy misteriosa-
    mente:
setenta y seis, setenta y ocho,
    ochenta.
¿Marca es de nuestro avance hacia
    la suma
total, esclavitud a una aritmética

que nos escolta, pertinaz pareja
de pares y de impares,
recordando a los pájaros
esta forzosa lentitud del hombre?

¿O son, como los años, tantas
    cifras
señas con que marcar en la
    carrera
sin señales del tiempo, a cada
    vida
las lindes del aliento,
año de cuna, año de tumba,
    texto
sencillo de dos fechas
que cabe en cualquier losa de
    sepulcro?
¿Llegaré hasta qué número?
    Quizá
tú no sabes tampoco adonde
    acabas.
Tu número cien mil, si tú
    pudieras
prolongarte, ya muerta, sin tus
    casas,
seguir, por el espacio, así derecha

¿no sería la Arcadia, y dos
    amantes,
a la siesta tendidos en la grama,

with drops of electric dew.
Infinite to the eye
and all numbered, with ev-
    ery step
you reveal us a something,
two by two, most mysteri-
    ously:
seventy-six, seventy-eight,
    eighty.
Is it the mark of our advance
    toward the total
sum, an enslavement to an
    arithmetic
that escorts us, obstinate pair
of evens and odds,   20
reminding the birds
of this inescapable slowness
    of man?
Or are so many ciphers, like
    years,
signpo s on the unknown
    course
of each of our lives, mark-
    ing
the limits of our breath,
the year of the cradle, year
    of the tomb, plain
text of two dates
that fits on any gravestone?
What number will I reach?   30
    Perhaps
even you do not know where
    you end.
Your number one hundred
    thousand, if you could
prolong yourself, after death,
    without your houses,
to continue through space, so
    straightly,
wouldn't it be Arcadia, and
    two lovers,
resting on the lawn of their
    siesta,

antes de Cristo y de los
rascacielos?
Nunca respondes, hasta que es
de noche,
cuando en lo alto de tus dos
orillas
empiezan los eléctricos avisos   40
a sacudir las almas indecisas.
"¡Lucky Strike, Lucky Strike!"
¡Qué refulgencia!
¿Y todo va a sér eso?

¿Un soplo entre los labios,
imitación sin canto de la música,
tránsito de humo a nada?

¿Naufragaré en el aire, sin
tragedia?
Ya desde la otra orilla, otros
destellos
me alumbran otra oferta:

"White Horse. Caballo blanco."   50
¿Whiskey? No.
Sublimación, Pegaso.
Dócil sirviente antiguo de las
musas,
ofreciendo su grupa de botella,

al que encuentre el estribo que
le suba.
¿Cambiaré el humo aquél por tu
poema?
¡Cuántas más luces hay, más hay
de dudas!

Tu piso, sí, tu acera, están muy
claros,
pero rayos se cruzan en tus crestas

y el aire se me vuelve laberinto,

sin más hilo posible que aquí   60
abajo:

before Christ and sky-
scrapers?
You never answer, until
nighttime,
when at the top of your two
shores
the electric signs begin
to jolt hesitant souls.
"Lucky Strike, Lucky Strike!"
What splendor!
And that's what it is all
about?

A puff between two lips,
a songless mimicry of music,
a transit from smoke to
nothing?

Will I be shipwrecked in the
air, without tragedy?
But from the other shore,
other sparkles
offer me another enlighten-
ment:

"White Horse. White Horse."
Whiskey? No.
Sublimation, Pegasus.
Tame ancient servant of the
muses,
offering the rump of his
bottle
to whoever finds the stirrup
to mount him.
Should I exchange the puff
of smoke for his poem?
However many lights there
are, there are more
doubts!

Your pavement, yes, your
sidewalk, is very clear,
but streaks crisscross on your
crests
and the air becomes a labyrinth
with no possible thread but
the one here below,

el hilo de un tranvía sin Ariadna.

*¡Qué fácil, sí, perderse en una
    recta!*
Nace centelleante, otra divisa,

*un rumbo más, y confusión
    tercera:*
*"¡Dientes blancos, cuidad los
    dientes blancos!"*
*Se abre en la noche una sonrisa
    inmensa*
dibujada con trazos de bombillas

*sobre una faz supuesta en el
    espacio.*
*¡Tan bien que me llevabas por tu
    asfalto,*
*cuando no me ofrecías tus
    anuncios!*
*Ahora, al mirarlos, no hay nada
    seguro,*
*para las mariposas, que se
    queman*
*un millar por minuto en torpes
    aras.*
*No sé por dónde voy más que
    en el suelo.*

*Y, sin embargo, el alba no se
    alquila.*
*Lo malo son las luces, las
    hechizas*
luces, las ignorantes pitonisas

*que responden con voces más
    oscuras*
a las oscuras voces que pedían.
Y otra surge,
*más trágica que todas: "Coca-
    Cola.*
*La pausa que refresca." Pausa.
    ¿En dónde?*
¿La de Paolo y Francesca en su

the thread of a streetcar
    without Ariadne.
How very easy to be lost on
    a straight line!
Another emblem is born
    twinkling,
one direction more, and a
    third confusion:
"White teeth, take care of
    your white teeth!"
An immense smile opens in
    the night
drawn with little lightbulb
    traces
on a face superimposed in
    space.
How well you led me over
    your asphalt

70   before you offered me your
    announcements!
Now, seeing them, nothing
    is sure,
for the butterflies who burn
    out
a thousand a minute on
    clumsy altars.
I don't know where I am go-
    ing, except that it is on
    the ground.
And yet, the dawn could
    never be bought off.
The evil is the lights, the
    bewitching
lights, the ignorant sorcer-
    esses
who give the dark voices that
    asked, darker answers.

80   Another surges,
    the most tragic of all: "Coca-
    Cola.
    The pause that refreshes." A
    Pause. Where?
    The pause of Paulo and Fran-

lectura?
¿La del Crucificado entre dos
  mundos,
muerte y resurrección? O la otra,
  ésta,
la nada entre dos nadas: el
  domingo.
Van derechos los pasos todavía:

quebrada línea, avanza, triste, el
  alma:
tu falsa rectitud no la encamina.

Fingiendo una alegría de arco iris

pluricolor se enciende otra divisa:
"Gozad del mundo. Hoy, a las
  ocho y treinta."
La van a defender cien bailarinas

con la precisa lógica de un cuerpo

que argumenta desnudo por el
  aire
mientras las coristas,
con un ritmo de jazz, van
  repitiendo
aquel sofisma, aquel, aquel
  sofisma.
¿A eso llevabas? ¿El final, tan
  simple?
¿Vale la pena haber llegado al
  número
seiscientos veintisiete,
y encontrarse otra vez con nues-
  tros padres?
Mas no será. Ya el príncipe constante,
que vuelve, si se fue, que no se
  rinde,
con su grito de guerra: "Dientes
  blancos,
no hay nada más hermoso," nos
  avisa,

cesca in their reading?
Of the crucified Christ between two worlds,
death and resurrection? Or
  the other, this one,
the nothing between two
  nothingnesses: Sunday.
And the steps still go directly on:

a broken line, the soul, steps
  sadly forward:
your false rectitude does not
  guide her.

90 Pretending a multicolor rainbow
joy, another emblem gleams:
"Enjoy the world. Today, at
  eight-thirty."
A hundred ballerinas are going to defend it
with the exact logic of one
  body
in naked debate across the
  air,
while the chorus girls,
in jazz time, keep repeating

that sophism, that ultimate
  sophism.
That's where you're headed?
  Just to the end?

100 Is it worth having reached
  the number
six hundred twenty-seven,
to be with our parents
  again?
But no. The constant prince,

who returns, if he ever left,
  who will not surrender,
with his war cry: "White
  teeth,
nothing is lovelier," signals
  us,

contra la gran tramoya

que no se cansan de cantar los
    besos.
El dentífrico salva:
meditación, mañana tras mañana,   110

al verse en el espejo el esqueleto;

cuidarlo bien. Los huesos nunca
    engañan,
y ellos han de heredar lo que
    dejemos.
Ellos, puro resumen de Afrodita,

poso final del sueño.

                            Ya no sigo.
Incrédulo de letras y de aceras

me sentaré en el borde de la una

a esperar que se apaguen estas
    luces
y me dejen en paz, con las   120
    antiguas.
Las que hay detrás, publicidad
    de Dios,
Orión, Cefeo, Arturo, Casiopea,

anunciadoras de supremas
    tiendas,
con ángeles sirviendo
al alma, que los pague sin
    moneda,
la última, sí, la para siempre
    moda,
de la final, sin tiempo, primavera.

against the great stage arti-
    fice,
that kisses never tire of sing-
    ing.
Dentifrice saves:
meditation, morning after
    morning,
seeing its skeleton in the
    mirror;
take good care of it. Bones
    never deceive
and it is they who will in-
    herit whatever we leave.
They, the pure epitome of
    Aphrodite,
the final rest, the sediment
    of sleep.
                        I can't go on.
Incredulous with letters and
    with sidewalks,
I will sit down on the edge
    of one
to wait until these lights
    go off
to leave me alone, with the
    ancient ones.
Those behind them, God's
    publicity,
Orion, Cepheus, Arcturus,
    Cassiopeia,
announcers of supreme
    stores,
with angels waiting on
the soul, who will pay them
    without coin,
the last, yes, the perpetual
    style
of the final, timeless
    spring.) *

The setting for the poem is clearly identifiable as the center
of New York City, described in the course of a walk which takes
the protagonist down Broadway to Times Square. The poem's

title refers to the square's gigantic electric signs, flashing adver-
tising messages to the nocturnal passersby. An imagined dialogue
begins, as the poet addresses the city, in feigned awe, as the
supreme monument of the twentieth century. The city is personified as an ascetic, standing proud and erect, sure of himself
and of his course in life. In this role, the city also symbolizes
America, in its self-assured role as a world leader, crusader for
democracy and freedom, and, at the end of the second world
war, as the mightiest power on earth.

The tone of the poet's address is clearly ironic; not one of
admiration, as the initial verses might at first lead one to
suppose, but one of scorn for materialistic values expressed in
exact quantities and numbers. These first three verses are full
of connotations. The reference to asceticism is an allusion to the
country's puritanism. The stiff rectilinear forms of the buildings
stand for America's self-righteousness, which comes from considering financial wealth almost as a reward for virtue.

The image of the city street as an artificial stream, and of the
skyscrapers as substitutes for riverbanks, already appeared, as
we have seen in "Man Standing on the Shore." This supreme
creation of modern man is but a poor copy of nature. As the
protagonist continues his walk along the numbered streets,
it becomes a symbol of every man's journey through life, which
contemporary society has grown accustomed to evaluate only in
terms of measurable accomplishments. The city could well be
deceiving itself, could be measuring the void; the labyrinth of
empty lives in which birth and death are mere signposts in the
endless course of time (23-29). The last question (30-37) about
the city's, and civilization's, final destiny is also ironic. Man's
basic dilemma: the search for a meaningful victory against
death, and a real purpose to his life, has not changed in spite
of modern technical feats. Science has not given man an answer
to this problem, and so, contemporary man's dilemma is still
the same as that which faced his distant forefathers: Adam and
Eve upon leaving Eden (36-38). The poet imagines the city's
answer, in the form of its luminous messages, to this basic
question of the ultimate meaning of life (38-41).

The tone of the poem changes in the second part from irony
to sarcasm, as the protagonist receives and judges the messages

of the neon signs. A cigarette ad, a bright puff of smoke, symbolizes nothingness and the tragic boredom of city life. A liquor ad, an invitation to pleasure, offers a false Pegasus, leading not to poetry, but to the escape afforded by alcoholism. The poet is taken aback and begins to lose faith in this "rectilinear truth." As each message brings added doubts, the night filled with light appears to him as a labyrinth filled with contradicting paths (56-61). The toothpaste ad, in the form of a faceless smile, stands for the obsessive cult of youth, the cult of the body—of pure matter—without ultimate end. The Coca-Cola sign advocates "the pause that refreshes." But will this be a momentous pause, one of the great moments in the history of culture, such as the one immortalized by Dante's great lovers, or by Christ's three-day pause between death and resurrection? Hardly! It is an empty pause filled with *ennui*, the pause on a Sunday afternoon, which brings man to the inevitable contemplation of his empty life (80-86).

Briefly, the Radio City Music Hall ad launches a pathetic call to its escapist pleasures. The poet understands that of all of the city's messages, the dentifrice ad alone offers a lasting truth: "take good care of your teeth," have respect for those bones which will one day be all that remains of the beauty of youth (103-15). The only lasting value in this materialistic world is thus death.

Like a modern Fray Luis de León, Salinas' reaction is one of *contemptu mundi*: Escape from Reality. He will trade the jagged rhythms of the signs for the eternal music of the heavens (116-28). His contemplation symbolizes a return to nature and spiritual life, to the eternal Spring evoked in the last verse; beautiful interior life, as described in another poem, "Contra esta primavera" ("Against This Spring"), whose meaning and place in *All Things Made Clearer* I have already discussed.

The use of so many cultural references in this and other poems of *All Things Made Clearer* is in itself a reminder that, if they seem somehow quaintly out of place when dealing with present-day reality, it is because in the pursuit of strictly materialistic aims man has lost touch with the great myths of the past, and with the spiritual aims and dreams they represented. Salinas thus could not have chosen a more appropriate medium

to convey his lamenting commentary on the dangers of contemporary values to the proper spiritual evolution of man.

V   Confidence: *The Final Acceptance of Reality*

The poems of *Confidence* are mostly Nature poems; descriptions of the small treasures—a rosebud, a cloud, a bird—which
bring us a daily share of beauty and enjoyment. After conclud-
ing *All Things Made Clearer*, reading through *Confidence* has
a soothing effect. There is not a trace of doubt in any of the
twenty-four poems, and only one, "Extraños" ("Strangers"), p.
766, reflects the fears expressed in the previous book. When
Salinas is no longer faced with the threatening surroundings of
urban life, he simply returns to his basic attitude of, first of
all, enjoying the present, and intuiting a basic order in the
potential perfection of the future. *Confidence* is the book which
best expresses Salinas' instinctive reactions in coping with everyday life. His philosophical system still comes into play, but only
in the background as a muted justification for his enthusiasm
for life. This system explains why, unlike in the nature poems
of the first period, Salinas no longer expresses disappointment
in the passing of each moment. Seen not from the point of view
of any mortal individual, but as the manifestation of a total
cosmic embrace, the material world is no longer an illusion.

I will limit my discussion to the mention of a few key poems
which contain Salinas' clearest statements on how to live happily
in life. "En un trino" ("Within a Bird-trill"), p. 733, tells how
the poet has found happiness in a generous giving of himself,
in communion with nature, without ulterior motive:

Soy feliz en el aire,	(I am happy, within the air
dejándome en sus brazos	surrendering to its [lulling] arms,
volar a donde ellos [i.e., *los*	to fly wherever they [the birds]
pájaros] *vuelen*	might take me
a sus rumbos, sin clave,	in their spontaneous aimless flights
mejores que mis pasos.	more meaningful than my own steps.
. . . .	. . . .
Ahora voy, retirándome	I shall go on withdrawing
ya de mí, hacia vosotros,	from myself, and joining you,

inevitables sabios *del aire, por el aire.* *Feliz seré mirando* *a las felicidades*	inevitable sages of the air, in the air. I shall be happy contemplating the murmuring and swiftly mov- ing
que susurran, que vuelan *de la rama y del pájaro,* *lentamente olvidado* *de mí, ya sin memoria.*	happinesses of the branch and of the bird, slowly losing all awareness of myself, devoid of memory.
. . . . *Lo que yo no acerté* *otros me lo acertaron.*	. . . . And what I did not attain others attained for me.)

(pp. 733-34)

The feelings expressed in this poem show what degree of "decentralization of the self" the poet has reached, and to what extent he now feels himself in communion with the greater "Thou," the integral and universal "sea of love."

In "Presente simple" ("Simple Present"), p. 745, Salinas returns to the mood of *The Contemplated Sea* in which exterior reality and vision coincided perfectly in an immutable present: *Ni recuerdos, ni presagios:/ sólo el presente cantado . . . Ni vida ni muerte, nada:/ sólo el amor, sólo amando* (Neither memories, nor presages:/ only the singing present . . . Neither life nor death, nothing:/only love, only loving).

"Ver lo que veo" ("Seeing what I see"), p. 777, should dispel once and for all the view of Salinas as a Neoplatonic dreamer. The dreaming "I" of *All Things Made Clearer* and the living man are no longer in opposition, as Salinas explicitly rejects the need for any idealist search:

Quisiera más que nada, más que
*   sueño,*
ver lo que veo.
No buscar hondos signos por
*   celestes*
mundos supremos.
	(I want, more than any other
	    thing, more than a dream,
	to see what I see.
	Not to search for deep signs in
	    celestial
	higher realms.

. . . . *A ti te acerca tu presente. Ser* *es estar siendo.*	. . . . Your present offers itself to you. To be is to be alive.
. . . .	. . . .

Por la visión de lo que está delante *dejo el proyecto.*	For the vision of what's before me I abandon my search.
. . . .	. . . .
Sí. Ver lo que se ve. Ya está el poema, *aquí, completo.* (pp. 777-79)	Yes. To see what we see. The poem's already before us, complete.)

The last poem (p. 780), which gives its name to the book, was according to A. Debicki[13] probably inspired by Bécquer's "Rima IV." Some of the stanzas of Bécquer's poem seem particularly appropriate for Salinas' purpose in a justification of poetry as reflecting man's eternal spiritual search as opposed to the materialistic solutions of science:

> *Mientras la ciencia no alcance*
> *las fuentes de la vida,*
> *y en el mar o en el cielo haya un abismo*
> *que al cálculo resista;*
>
> . . . .
>
> *¡Habrá poesía!*

> (As long as science cannot bring itself to discover
> the fountains of life,
> and while in the sea and the sky there is an abyss
> which defies all calculation,
>
> . . . .
>
> There will be poetry!)

Like Béquer, Salinas sees his poetic mission as a necessary counterweight in reminding modern man that not everything can be reduced to measurable atoms, and that the death of each material element, and of each individual, does not necessarily mean its complete annihilation, since it can be reincarnated in future perfections. Poetry will be:

Memoria que le convenza *a esta tarde que se muere* *de que nunca estará muerta*	(A memory which might convince an afternoon that's slowly dying that it will never really die
. . . .	. . . .
Mientras haya	While there remains

| *lo que hubo ayer, lo que hay hoy* | what existed yesterday, what still remains today |
| *lo que venga.* (pp. 781-82) | and what will come tomorrow.) |

The last known poem written by Salinas, in the midst of great physical suffering from the disease which was to take his life two months later, still expresses the same unwavering faith. The poem, dated September 28, 1951, is entitled "Futuros" ("Futures"), and its last stanza is very much in the spirit of *Confidence*:

En la cima del pasado	(In the past's crest one can hear
cantando el futuro está.	the future already singing.
Calla y óyele: ya es tuyo.	Be silent, and listen: it is yours.
Porque todo acaba en a. (p. 799)	Because everything ends in *a*.)

CHAPTER 6

Prose and Theater (1941-1951)

THE last decade of Salinas' life was his most productive, due perhaps to the relative social isolation in which he lived as an exile in a foreign culture, but also to the excellent working conditions which he encountered in the American academic world. Besides the poetry already discussed, books published in close succession included a volume of sociological essays, his two most important studies in literary criticism, on Rubén Darío and Jorge Manrique, his novel *The Incredible Bomb*, and short stories joined under the title of *El desnudo impecable y otras narraciones* (*The Impeccable Nude and Other Stories*). His theater, which remained unpublished during his lifetime, was also written during this period. Because they provide an interesting ideological and personal background for other works of this period, the essays on modern life will be discussed first.

I *In Defense of Culture*

The five essays published under the title of *El defensor* (*The Defender*) were probably conceived as lectures and written during Salinas' stay in Puerto Rico, beginning in the summer of 1942. The last one, entitled "Defensa del lenguaje" ("In Defense of Language"), was in fact a baccalaureate address delivered at the University of Puerto Rico in 1944.[1] These early dates should be noted in appraising the author's analysis of certain basic ills in contemporary society, which might not have been as apparent to the ordinary observer as they are indeed evident today. The essays were first published in book form by the National University of Colombia in 1948. That year marked the beginning of a prolonged period of political instability and civil strife in that country, with disastrous conse-

133

quences to its literary and cultural life. As a result, most of the copies of Salinas' book were never distributed and were eventually destroyed. Only with the printing of a second edition in 1967 did the importance of these essays fully come to light.

Most of all, they are of interest because, as Juan Marichal tells us in his prologue to the second edition, they reveal a previously hidden "surface personality" or spontaneous social self. Salinas shares his likes and dislikes, and demonstrates his keen observation of contemporary American life, as well as a wealth of information on a surprising variety of current subjects. To read *The Defender* is, in a sense, to be introduced to the congenial conversationalist so highly esteemed by all who knew him. Salinas himself prized this spontaneity and did not revise or edit these texts prior to publication, allowing some repetitions to remain as emphasis upon what he considered to be his most pressing social concerns. As the title implies, and as we are told in the foreword, these essays were prompted by a deep sense of alarm at the weakening of "certain essential and traditional forms of spiritual life"[2] which the author believed was his and every civilized man's duty to defend as best he could.

All five essays deal with changing attitudes toward the various manifestations of language in social intercourse: conversation, reading, letter writing. The author deals with each of these aspects separately, but the larger context of his discussion is a general denunciation of the misuse of science and technology, when placed at the service of strictly materialistic aims. Salinas' accusation does not, of course, originate strictly with him, and on various occasions he quotes well-known sources—such as Lewis Mumford's *Technics and Civilizations*—to reinforce his arguments.

A few central ideas repeated throughout the essays can be summarized as follows: The beginning of a radical change in civilization coincided, in the Industrial Age, with the regimentation of time. Time, like money, became a commodity to be utilized to the fullest, in the sole pursuit of material gain and the physical conquest of the environment. Eventually, even this purpose was forgotten, and the race against time became a value in itself. The author speaks of the psychosis of time—the morbid fear of wasting time—or of the idolatry of time. The contemporary Tartuffe, says Salinas, does not pride himself on his virtues, but on his ever increasing time-consuming tasks.[3] His moments of leisure are spent in frenetic activity. This point is then illustrated with a satire of golf playing and with a comic description of up-to-date daily occupations as listed in a current women's magazine. Salinas concludes that man's whole life has become caught in a frenetic pace of self-fulfilling action.

This dynamic conception of existence has gradually reduced man's potential for meaningful reflection and social interaction. Individuals have become increasingly isolated from their fellow-men and have lost all sense of a cultural bond with them or with past generations, as well as any feeling of responsibility toward future ones. Therein lies, for Salinas, the real menace, the suicidal threat, for the future of humanity. The modern fetishes of time, efficiency, and material success have resulted in man's inability to see beyond the scope of his own individual boundaries. For a contemporary man, life can only be *his* life. Collectively, modern society could well repeat Louis XV's famous saying: "After us, the deluge."[4]

Salinas concludes that only the reestablishment of an historical conscience can restore in man "his pride in being transitory." The noblest duty of each individual is to do his share in assuring the preservation of the link between past and future, in a total and cumulative cultural heritage.[5] In this idea, especially the paradoxical praise of transitoriness, we find a reiteration of the faith in a collective rather than individual fulfillment which we have seen expressed in Salinas' late poetry.

If this critique of contemporary life is included in a series of essays on language, it is because Salinas saw in changing attitudes toward the spoken and written word one of the surest signs of a lessening of the spiritual quality of life. Modern society has lost its sense of respect toward language, which has been reduced to the status of a technical tool, nothing more. The emphasis on efficiency and speed has reduced verbal exchanges to such an extent that in comparison with previous generations, ours is losing its dominion over language as even a barely functional means of self-expression. A great deal of the so-called problem of communication finds its origin in this phenomenon. Salinas notes the avoidance at almost any cost

of meaningful exchanges in conversation, and the decline of
letter writing, except in strictly conventional and impersonal
formulae which he aptly calls "canned letters." Another sign—
and cause—of the deterioration of language is the growing
reliance on visual devices such as billboards and neon signs.
Salinas wrote this essay before the age of television which would
bring out even more this overreliance on visual, one-way communication and its consequent isolation of the individual.

Two essays, "Defensa de la lectura" ("In Defense of Reading") and "Defensa de la minoría literaria" ("In Defense of a
Literary Minority"), deal with the disappearance of reading as
an art, and the diminishing role of literature. For Salinas, literature has traditionally performed two essential functions. First,
it mirrors the evolution of language. Second, it serves as a
repository of the experiences and conflicts of the past, allowing
us thereby to participate in it, and in the long tradition which
forms what Northrop Frye has termed the "myths of concern"
of Western civilization.[6] The deliberate cultivation of the art
of reading and the study of literature are therefore essential
in a humanistic society.

However, the contemporary attitude toward the written word
has been somewhat of an ironic paradox. Today, libraries are
larger than ever and compulsory education has extended reading skills to an ever greater percentage of the population. But
once again, the concern with speed and efficiency has made of
the modern reader what Salinas calls a total or partial neo-
illiterate. His reading is confined to matters of strict practical
information or of narrow professional interest. Among these
neo-illiterates Salinas includes scientific specialists, most poli-
ticians, and not a few academic scholars. He also satirizes the
magazine reader who can hardly keep up, from week to week,
with his incoming material. The scant leisure time still devoted
to reading is taken up with material of only actual or passing
interest, and with "escape" literature.

Salinas is particularly critical of the advent of the "best seller,"
marketed by reading clubs, and often deliberately chosen with
regard for what the majority of the public is apt to like and buy.
The democratization of reading may thus have already had an
adverse effect on the writing of new literature, especially fiction,

since tastes are now imposed by a passive majority, and not by an exploring cultural elite as in previous generations. The author also points to editions in "digest" form, and to filmed versions of literary works reduced to a mere story line (as well as to the invention of "classic comic"!) as further evidence that the tradition of reading as an art of re-creation (in the Unamunian sense of "creating anew") is all but forgotten.

II *"In Defense of Letter Writing"*

A discussion of *The Defender* would not be complete without some reference to the very personal form and style which elevate these seemingly informal discussions to the category of creative literary works. As a lecturer, Salinas combined the qualities of the natural teacher, the humanist, and the poet concerned not only with presenting facts, but, as always, with the intangible mystery behind these facts. He is also capable of blending many styles and moods—lyrical, humorous, satirical—either in delicate balance, or in abrupt contrast, for shock value. A good example of his rhetorical skill is provided in the book's longest apology, "Defensa de la carta misiva y de la correspondencia epistolar" ("In Defense of Letter Writing").

The essay begins with an indignant invective against the Western Union slogan, "Wire, don't write," which Salinas calls a dangerous example of subversion against civilized human communication. The essay proceeds in meandering form with frequent interruptions for anecdotes and personal asides. The basic thread is a brief history of epistolary exchanges, from the first known letter—a love letter written in Babylon, four thousand years ago—to correspondence in classical times, the first couriers and *messagers volants* of the Middle Ages and Renaissance, the first postal network in seventeenth-century France, the institution of the Penny Post (*ca.* 1840) in England (which for the first time made correspondence accessible to the masses and gave the country greater social unity) and, finally, the commercialization of letter writing in modern times. Also included in this fascinating account is a portrait gallery of famous secretaries through the ages, and a casual glance at the best-known manuals of epistolary style in most of Europe's major literatures. The

more serious topics, essential to Salinas' apology, appear inter-
twined within this narrative framework.

Of these the most important is the theory of the psychology
of letter writing: Salinas' exaltation of correspondence as a means
of crystallizing one's own feelings, and as a creative self-reckon-
ing with language when faced with the "moral" responsibility
of presenting a right image of oneself. The author also prizes
the necessary act of reflective communication in evoking a
mental picture of the friend to whom we address ourselves.
It is in this sense that a letter can be, as in Lope de Vega's
definition, "a mental prayer of absence," or that Salinas explains
the meaning of Donne's verse: "More than kisses, letters
mingle souls."[7]

Large sections of the essay are also devoted to character
studies of personalities behind famous correspondence. Salinas
speculates on the mixture of personal and creative motives which
prompted Madame de Sévigné to write her famous letters. He
also analyzes Lope de Vega's character as reflected in the courtly
advice concerning the conduct of sentimental adventures, which
he dispensed in his capacity as secretary to the Duke of Sessa.
In style and in the delicate attention to detail in drawing these
portraits, we are reminded of Salinas' contact with Proust, whom
he greatly admired and, as we have seen, had translated in
earlier years.

Finally, the same essay also provides a rare example of Salinas'
gifts as an art critic, in his remarks on the painting of Vermeer
van Delft. He, like Proust, greatly admired the Dutch painter
as an interpreter of subtle psychological moments arrested in
time. He analyzes the "poetry of absence" evoked in Vermeer's
two renditions of "The Reader," commenting on the use of light,
the relationship between the artist's famous interiors and the
inner emotions of the young girl reading her lover's letter, as
well as the details used to give the impression of the absent
lover's tangible presence in the girl's mind.[8]

Chronologically, *The Defender* is the first book, the writing of
which antedates most of the poetry of *All Things Made Clearer*,
in which Salinas deals with contemporary historical reality.
Though his themes basically never change, they are in all the

later works most often conveyed through familiar situations of modern life.

III   *Satire and the Allegory of a Future World*

Total world destruction by bombing, which Salinas had envisioned as a nightmarish fantasy in "Zero," became a very real possibility less than a year after the composition of that poem, with the dropping of the atom bomb. Salinas was so shaken by that event that he later wrote a play, *Caín, o una gloria científica* (*Cain, or a Glory of Science*), in which the inventor of the bomb has himself killed rather than lend his services to the preparation of the inevitable hecatomb.

By 1950, it was clear that the hard-won peace following the second World War was only a precarious calm, undermined by an atmosphere of fear and distrust which seemed to leave little hope for the future, A few months before his death, Salinas declared in an interview that he had recently felt compelled to write *The Incredible Bomb* "moved by the constant anguish of the present historical moment."[9] This novel is thus to be read as a personal message of protest against the mounting escalation of the "cold war," and in general, against the state of mind which regards periodic armed conflicts as inevitable. In the process, the author also sounds a renewed warning against man's enslavement by science, which could well lead to monstrous utopias such as those described in Huxley's *Brave New World* or Orwell's *1984*.

Like Huxley's novel, *The Incredible Bomb* is a fictional projection into the future; in this case, by a mere fifteen years. Since the future society envisioned by Salinas coincides in some details with that of *The Brave New World* at an early stage of its development, the two novels have been compared by several critics.[10] Such a comparison, however, can only be a superficial one. Huxley's approach is ironic, but at the same time it suggests a plausible anticipation of endurable life in the future. His novel seems to be based on real scientific theories, carried to realistic conclusions. Salinas' novel, which he called *fabulación*, is by contrast pure fantasy. It begins as a humorous satire filled with completely preposterous details. Then, rather unexpectedly, it becomes a poetic allegory, with details of plot and character development acceptable only on a symbolic level.

On the surface, the mythical island state of E.T.C. (the Spanish initials for Technological Scientific State) is still a democracy, with a parliament, an anachronistic constitutional ruler, and freedom of the press. But the government is already in the hands of an elite of technocrats who, through subtle mind conditioning and relentless slogans, have made great progress toward shaping a new society based on strictly scientific principles. Their ultimate goal is the elimination of all subjective responses, and the establishment of completely predictable and standardized patterns of human behavior. All pseudo-disciplines —those such as literature and history—not backed by empirical experimentations have been eliminated from educational programs. The Scientific Language Academy has abolished all imprecise words, all those charged with emotional content, like "catastrophe," or scientifically subversive, such as "imponderable." Behavioral and dietetic habits have been transformed: Food is now produced scientifically for a perfectly balanced and controlled diet. To combat old vices like alcoholism, a new nectar has been invented, identical in taste to wine, but with a soothing effect on the nerves. Like the "soma" in Huxley's novel, it also gives excellent results toward "social conditioning."

The scientific state keeps the vastest arsenals ever assembled, but is committed to use them only for the preservation of peace. So great is the commitment to peace that the word "war" is now considered archaic. There are only periods of "static peace," alternating with brief campaigns of "dynamic peace-keeping," to preserve justice and prevent tyranny. In view of this change, the war museum, center of the Acropolis of Science, has been renamed "The Rotunda of Peace."

There, one day, a mysterious bomblike object is discovered in the midst of the bomb collection. Although it is lodged in a glass case identical to all the others, no one is able to explain its clandestine appearance. The presumed bomb is oblong in shape and reddish-purple in color. It emits pounding sounds, and heaves like a breast. After a preliminary investigation is marred by the baffling death of several "indirect victims" of the bomb, it is decided that the object should be delivered for testing to a special commission of the state's highest-ranking scientists. However, despite experiments repeated hundreds of times, even the most precise instruments are found incapable of registering the simplest factors of weight, temperature, or sound waves. Tension mounts among government leaders, and as weeks pass a growing paranoia spreads to the masses. The Regent is obliged to declare a "state of irrationality," suppressing all further news, and lifting the official censure of long-forgotten diversions, like the reading of literary classics and the viewing of films.

Finally, in a frustrated fit of madness, the head scientist, Dr. Mendía, attacks the bomb with a knife, plunging it seven times into the purple mass, before taking his own life. From the bomb's seven wounds, strange sounds begin to emerge, imitating a whole range of heartrending human cries. In the form of pink bubbles, they fill the laboratory, break through its walls, and begin spreading like a gigantic atomic cloud over the countryside. No force is capable of checking its advance, inexorably paced at five kilometers per day. All mechanical devices are stopped on contact, and although plant and animal life appears unaffected, no human being can withstand for more than a few minutes the haunting sounds of suffering "which suffocate the soul." An immense exodus of people begins across the land; but when the pink clouds continue their advance across the ocean, it becomes apparent that no escape is possible and that the human race is apparently doomed.

At last, only two survivors remain on the island: Victor, an ex-journalist who had been serving a prison sentence for draft dodging, and Cecilia, the novel's protagonist, who had also been jailed for an alleged attempt on the life of one of the state's leaders. Cecilia belongs to an anachronistic remnant of the population as yet unconverted to the scientific creed. A few pockets of these fanatics still remained in the capital, especially in the medieval quarter surrounding the Gothic cathedral. Their views, including traditional religious beliefs, are now considered superstitions, but they have been tolerated in the name of democracy and also as a negative example, to show the scientifically

educated masses how much progress had been made over bar-
barism in just a few years.

Cecilia's anarchism and resistance to all campaigns of "dynamic
peace-keeping" had resulted from the profound effect caused
in her by the death of her brother, a bomber pilot in the last
world conflict, who had inexplicably gone mad and committed
suicide when returned to civilian life. Cecilia is able to endure
the effects of the incredible bomb precisely because, inwardly,
she has experienced some of its effects for many years.

Where science has failed, she intuits the secret of the bomb.
A strange comparison imposes itself on her mind between it
and the heart of the mourning Mother of Christ, the *Mater
Dolorosa,* as she is traditionally represented, with her heart
pierced with seven swords. Cecilia perceives that the so-called
bomb is a supernatural manifestation of collective grief, the
heart of humanity in rebellion against the cruelty of man
toward man, after centuries of stoic resignation:

*Todos los tiempos del matar, y los muertos de muchos siglos, se
juntaban aquí en pavorosa simultaneidad . . . Se negaba el dolor a
ser historia; aquí venía, en enorme masa secular, a que se le sintiera
vivo y presente por los hombres que viven recluídos en sus solas
vidas y no creen en más dolor que el del momento.* (p. 190)[11]

(The killings of all times, and the dead of so many centuries, were
joined here in awesome simultaneity. Suffering, refusing to become
part of history, manifested itself in the form of an enormous, ageless,
mass—alive and present—confronting men who have isolated themselves within their solitary lives and do not believe in any suffering
except that of the present moment.)

Moved by an irresistible feeling of pity, Cecilia makes her
way to the laboratory where the "bomb" has been abandoned
by the fleeing scientists. In an impulsive gesture, she embraces
the human heart. Immediately, the seven wounds close up and
the unbearable human cries gradually subside. Through Cecilia's
supreme act of love, the end of the world is averted, and a new
life can begin, ending in a true Utopia . . . "toward a world
free from the cry of Abel" (p. 191).

On the basis of the plot alone, especially its emotional ending, and its overt symbolism, the novel may seem to run the

danger of overstating its message. But in spite of being burdened with a certain amount of "preaching," it is successful in maintaining to the end a convincing fictional illusion. Its success probably lies in the balance between subtle satire in the first part, and the gradually emerging allegory which becomes explicit only late in the story and is then rapidly resolved, before it has a chance to degenerate into sentimental melodrama.

The first part of the novel remains the most satisfying. Initially, the story is told without emotional involvement or editorial comment on the part of the narrator. As Ricardo Gullón has pointed out, the satirical intention is conveyed solely through a falsely elegant, slightly pedantic journalistic style, full of archaisms and learned turns of phrases.[12] This stylistic medium makes the description of the new scientific order seem totally incongruous. By contrast, some of the characters express themselves in quaint popular speech, full of Madrid colloquialisms, which belies the State's attempt at standardization and regimentation of language. The clash between the two stylisic levels is in itself highly comic. There is also humor in many of the small details of the plot itself, such as the description of the fumbling police investigation, or the capricious turns of fate which frustrate the government's attempt to control "scientifically" a popular plebiscite concerning the fate of the bomb. On occasion, the author strikes a jarring tragicomic note, as with the absurd death of the museum director, electrocuted by a lie detector.

With respect to characterization, the novel's most serious defect is the handling of the central figures, especially Cecilia, who is little more than a lifeless mouthpiece for the author's ideas and feelings. Neither she nor Victor are psychologically developed. But the book abounds in well-observed and rapidly sketched types, such as the grotesque military leaders, the ministerial council, and the good-natured, slightly anachronistic regent.

The novelist succeeds in maintaining the necessary tension in his narrative by making use of detective-story techniques. Usually, a small intriguing detail at the end of a chapter serves as a catalyst for the next. The main element of suspense is provided, of course, by the speculations on the bomb's secret, which is not revealed until the very end of the novel. As in mystery novels, Salinas leads the reader along a succession of

deductive paths and conjectures, all of which ultimately prove
false. This is one of his favorite techniques, one which he also
uses in several short stories. It is the poet's way of expressing
his distrust of empirical proofs and of pointing out, as always,
the lack of substance in material reality.

IV *"Magical Realism" in Five Short Stories*

The Impeccable Nude, and Other Stories, the last of his works
which Salinas was to see in print, is a collection of five tales
which confirms his talent as a prose stylist, and reveals his
complete mastery of the short-story form. Salinas' handling of
language is truly extraordinary. As in the novel, he is capable
of striking many stylistic levels, including lyrical veins reminiscent of the Vanguardist prose in *On the Eve of Joy*. But the
choice of a particular style is always guided by the subject at
hand. Thus, in the first story, "El desayuno" ("The Breakfast"),
the same elegant style introduced in the novel is now used for
the description of the respectable faculty residence of a women's
Ivy League college. The very rhythm of the language gives one
an impression of quiet order and timeless respectability. The
description lingers on significant details, such as the portrait
of the founder—the image of a patron saint for whom a votive
lamp burns night and day—or the gilded statue of Mercury
which seems to preside over the daily afternoon teas, where
campus gossip is exchanged:

*Detrás del diván la imagen pseudo-broncínea de Mercurio, el divo
de las correturías, patrono de tráficos de toda laya, dejaba caer
alientos inspiradores sobre las dos venerables buhoneras, que con-
sagraban los que les quedaban, de días, a activos empleos mercuriales,
trapicheo de gacetillas y canje de chismes.* (p. 20)[13]

(Behind the sofa, the imitation-bronze statue of Mercury—god of
brokerage houses, patron saint of every imaginable trade—breathed
whiffs of inspiration upon the two venerable hawkers, who conse-
crated their remaining days to active mercurial pursuits, the scheming
of gossip columns, and the exchange of rumors.)

One of Salinas' particular traits is the use of metaphors for
psychological analysis. Thus, in "La gloria y la niebla" ("Glory
and Mist"), he describes as follows the inner conflicts of a

puritanical young American girl, whose instinctive attitude toward life is to repress all spontaneous feelings:

Varias horas llevaba Lena fortificándose; acumuladas tenía decisiones sobre decisiones, sillares de cantería moral, murallón para defenderse, no sabía bien de qué. Pero bastó una punta de acero, la de la plumilla con que Luis trazó sus palabras, para atravesar los engañosos lienzos y dejar al descubierto lo defendido, su corazón. (pp. 67-68)

(For several hours, Lena had been fortifying herself; she had accumulated decision upon decision, blocks of stone from the moral quarry, a thick wall of defense, though she wasn't certain against what. But it took a single point of steel—the little penpoint with which Luis traced his words—to pierce the illusory fabric and bare what she was protecting: her heart.)

Unlike in the novel, characters in the stories come alive as individuals, and not merely as conventional types or symbols. Mr. Turner, in "The Breakfast," is the perfect prototype of the "neo-illiterate," already satirized in *The Defender*. As manager of a large bookstore, he dutifully reads current best sellers, or at least reliable reviews, on every conceivable subject in order to be able to counsel his clients. His voracious reading takes up all his free time and provokes the admiration of his wife and of his customers. His reputation is that of an austere scholar, but this is only a façade which the author destroys with the following comment:

Su cabeza, a lo que más se parecía era a sólida tubería de material refractorio, por cuyos caños pueden pasar los mayores caudales, helados o ardientes, y ella no se deja comunicar pizca de humedad, ni se calienta cuando el agua corre calentísima, ni la más fría la refresca un grado. (p. 34)

(What his head most resembled was a solid pipeline of refractory material, through whose plumbing the greatest streams of water, cool and hot, can pass, while it never feels the slightest bit humid to the touch, nor gets warm when the water runs steaming hot, or even one degree cooler when it runs icy.)

But Mr. Turner also has a secret passion, hidden even from his wife: he is addicted to comic strips, which he devours twice a day, while commuting to and from work. The contrast between the solidity of this character's public personality and his shallow inner self is what transforms him from a type to an individual, with a credible human, and paradoxically even endearing, dimension.

Salinas' handling of structure, tempo, and mood is extremely versatile, and, like style, dictated by exigencies of theme. "Los inocentes" ("The Innocents"), for instance, is based on suspense and written like a detective story, while "Glory and Mist," whose title refers to the illusory pursuit of literary fame, is full of pathos. This story whose last scene is developed on a symbolic plane, is reminiscent of the allegorical technique used in the novel. The scene takes place in a San Francisco park where two lovers—Lena, the puritanical young American, and Luis, a promising Spanish writer—have taken refuge. In these surroundings shrouded in mist, they try to read the inscription on a statue honoring Edgar Allan Poe. Fate has it that the still controversial poet has been the object of a slander campaign from certain civic-minded ladies, blocking the completion of the monument. The pedestal stands empty, and this empty space, completely hidden in the fog, is the cause of the young man's fatal fall as he climbs up to read the inscription.

A comparable element of chance is common to all stories. Though each narrative takes as its point of departure perfectly credible everyday events, the intrusion of hazard or uncanny coincidences gives it a fantastic dimension. Salinas' manner might be said to recall what critics of contemporary Latin-American literature refer to as "magical realism," although the distortion of time and space which is a usual characteristic of this school is absent here, except in the last story. "Chance is the poetry of life," says the protagonist of "El autor novel" ("The Neophyte Author"), and facts alone, even methodically accumulated and considered impartially, can often lead to totally reversible conclusions.

The five tales thus have as a common theme Salinas' well-known preoccupation with the delusion of surface reality, and a defense of the imagination as a palliative against an inscrutable world order. A direct consequence of this inscrutability is the relativity of guilt and innocence[14]—the central concern of "The Breakfast" and "The Innocents." In the latter story, the protagonist wavers between testifying on behalf of a man accused of running over someone with his car, and betraying the confidence of the victim of the accident which, despite all the evidence, could well have been a suicide.

Two stories are condemnations of life-stifling ethics: puritan pragmatism and fear of sensuality in "Glory and Mist," and the equation of sex and female nudity with sin in the title story, "The Impeccable Nude." "The Neophyte Author" deals with the very Hispanic theme of envy and Cainite hatred, finally redeemed by the protagonist's discovery of pure altruistic love. This last tale is the most fantastic, due to the introduction of a supernatural element. Its title refers to a device of formal duplication by which the author-protagonist sees his own life and destiny first copied, then foreshadowed in a novel submitted to his critical opinion by an amateur novelist. As it turns out, this new author might possibly be a reincarnation of the Devil (called "el gran Maquinario"), and as such, the instigator of the consuming passion from which the protagonist must ultimately free himself. The protagonist of this story is the most fascinating figure in a long gallery of writers and intellectuals who, by voicing some typically Salinian ideas, clearly function as the author's "doubles."

In addition to repeating these traditional Salinian themes, this collection continues the criticism of contemporary life initiated in *All Things Made Clearer* and *The Defender*. Besides Mr. Turner, the "neo-illiterate," other types are satirized, such as the journalist in "The Innocents" (p. 193), and the strip-teaser in "The Impeccable Nude" (p. 118). The satire also surfaces in some descriptions: that of a modern airport in "Glory and Mist" (p. 66), and the equally expressionistic glance at New York's Central Park, in "The Impeccable Nude" (p. 152). Of all Salinas' nonpoetic works, the short stories are possibly his most original and formally well conceived. Had the author lived longer, he might well have acquired a reputation as a story writer as well as a poet.

V *A Poet's Concept of the Stage*

Salinas' theatrical production consists of twelve one-act plays, mostly comedies, and two full-length dramas, all written during

the last six years of his life. In this last stage of his career, the
theater seemed to be emerging as an increasingly important
medium for him, perhaps because, like prose fiction, it offered
possibilities for more complex and multifaceted presentations
of recurrent themes, hitherto treated only from the poet-protagonist's single viewpoint.

The author had great hopes for success as creator of a new
kind of lyrical dama, but felt particularly handicapped by his
enforced isolation in an alien culture where he lacked both an
audience and access to potential producers. Until just before
his death, he steadfastly refused to publish any of his plays,
because none had yet been produced, and he did not want them
to meet the sanction of a reading public only. During his trip
to Colombia and Peru, in 1947, he sought commitments from
commercial producers for the staging of some of his one-act
plays. He received several promises, but as nothing came of
them, he blamed his lack of success on the base demands of
commercialism.[15] Finally, in February, 1951, a comedy entitled
La fuente del arcángel (*The Fountain of the Archangel*) was
staged at Columbia University, by the Spanish theater group of
Barnard College. This premiere performance was a notable
event, attended by Spanish exiles, friends, and distinguished
Hispanists from all over the eastern United States. Dámaso
Alonso, who was seated next to Salinas, gave a touching account
of the evening, describing the poet's visible excitement and
emotion at seeing his creation finally completed in time and
space.[16]

Since Salinas' death, however, only a few of his plays have
been produced, always by amateur or student groups.[17] Whereas
his poetry has received increased critical acclaim, especially in
recent years, his theater remains mostly forgotten. In spite of the
fact that an authoritative edition of the *Teatro completo* has been
available since 1957, the three most extensive studies dealing
with Salinas' theater—those of Edith Helman, Mario Maurín,
and J. Rodríguez Richart[18]—remain based on the 1952 edition
of the three plays which the author selected at the persistent
request of a Spanish editor, when he became aware of his
incurable illness.

A possible explanation for this theater's lack of success is that

Salinas, because he was working in such a vacuum, never became attuned to the dramatic medium and failed to exploit fully the visual and dynamic potentials of the stage. The parallel with Lorca comes to mind. By the time Lorca wrote his major plays, he had had ample training as an actor and director. He also strove to create a new poetic theater, but conceived it as a multidimensional spectacle, directed to all the senses. By contrast, Salinas tends to rely almost exclusively on verbal communication, and although his language is always magnificently evocative, it is the voice of the lyric poet that we tend to hear, not that of his characters.

The few visual devices that the author uses almost always strike one as unconvincing, even in a nonrealistic play. One example is his use, in no less than four plays, of alternate parallel scenes, in which one set of characters performs the action on one level, while another group of actors, though present, must pretend to ignore what is going on beside them. Usually, this is supposed to represent the two levels of everyday reality and fantasy. The only time this device is truly successful is in a scene from *The Fountain of the Archangel,* where the secondary action takes place on a puppet stage seen through a picture hanging on the back wall. The action on the puppet stage represents the heroine's dream world, while the world of staid social conventions and "common sense" is personified in the characters evolving in the foreground.

For this and another early play, Salinas turned to the long tradition of *costumbrista* or "genre" theater which portrays the local customs and speech of particular regions of Spain. *The Fountain of the Archangel* takes place in an Andalusian village around 1900, while in *La estratoesfera* (*The Stratosphere*)—subtitled *Tavern Scenes in One Act*—the stage set reproduces a typical Madrid café. The latter play has all the flavor of a popular sketch or *sainete* by Carlos Arniches or José López Silva, two Madrid *costumbristas* whom Salinas greatly admired. Possibly because of their folksy flavor, these two plays have been the most readily accepted, and in the case of the first, one of the most often produced.

Most of Salinas' comedies, however, are framed in conventional contemporary settings: a bourgeois salon, a hotel room, a res-

taurant, a city park. Except for the protagonists, his characters
are also the ordinary types of bourgeois comedy. Initially, the
action points to a world with which a modern spectator might
readily be able to identify. Once the public is comfortably
settled in familiar surroundings, a "magic transformation" is
attempted by means of techniques which Edith Helman rightly
compares with a prestidigitator's tricks.[19]

In a few plays, a surprise element which transforms a credible
world into one of shadows and illusions is introduced suddenly,
with hardly any preparation. The initial situation of *El precio*
(*The Price*), for example, reflects Salinas' fondness for detective intrigues. This case revolves around the identity of an
amnesiac young girl, possibly implicated in an unsolved murder.
The principal characters are a psychiatrist, his daughter Alicia,
and Melisa, the mystery girl, who a few days before was found
walking aimlessly by the side of the road. The only clue to the
fact that the heroine might be existing on a different plane from
the rest of the characters is given in the stage directions which
accompany her first appearance on stage: *Alta, delgada, vestirá
algo como bata de color claro, con el cabello suelto sobre el
hombro, sus pasos y sus modales han de revelar cierta arritmia,
unas veces rápidos, otras lentos"* (p. 197).[20] (Tall, slender, she
should wear a kind of light-colored robe, with her hair hanging loose on her shoulders; her steps and gestures should suggest
a certain lack of rhythm, quick-paced at times, and slow at
others.) We are also told that hers is a "spiritual beauty," in
contrast with Alicia's more sensual one. Melisa fascinates everyone she meets with her habit of calling people and things by
new poetic names and her ability to find beauty in the most
trivial objects.

The suspense over Melisa's identity is sustained until the
last scene, which ends with a rather contrived Pirandellian
solution. Melisa turns out to be not a real being of flesh and
blood, but a character escaped from a novel. When her creator
reclaims her, she recovers her identity but also "dies," having
lost the independent will by which she reshaped the world to
the measure of her imagination. Only the example of her temporary rebellion against a predetermined destiny remains, perhaps
as a temptation for the remaining characters, especially Alicia.

In *La isla del tesoro* (*Treasure Island*), one of the three plays selected for publication by Salinas, the initial situation is again a simple one. Marú, the heroine, is, like Melisa, a dreaming joyful girl impatient with her daily routine and always ready to transform life into a game. She has come to the capital in the company of her mother, a prospect which she seems to accept more with resignation than genuine enthusiasm. By chance, the previous occupant of her room was a young man who had committed suicide by jumping out the window to the canal below. The guest's identity is the hotel manager's well-guarded secret, but from the conversation between chambermaids in Scene One, we learn that he might have been a dispossessed nobleman or a disenchanted prince.

There is no "bombshell" in this play. The action unfolds according to a set of plausible and rather commonplace coincidences, and the fantastic dimension is introduced through the poetic observations which accompany Marú's daydreams. It was perhaps this play, more than any other, which led Mario Maurín to suggest the parallel between Salinas' style and theater technique and that of his French contemporary, Jean Giraudoux.[21] Thus, the discovery of the young suicide's diary in a bureau drawer is foreshadowed by Marú's remark:

Toda habitación de hotel decente es una isla. Rodeada de agua por todas partes, en cañerías, en tubos, en radiadores, claro. Segura, protegida contra el mundo. En toda isla comme il faut, *hay un tesoro escondido. ¡Buscad, y encontraréis!* (p. 104)

(In a respectable hotel, every room is an island. Surrounded by water on all sides, in plumbing pipes, in tubes, in radiators, of course. Secure and protected against the world. In every island worthy of the name there is a hidden treasure. Seek, and you shall find!)

The diary is a revelation for Marú, since in its contents she finds the exact expression of her own illusions and secret hopes, while the young man appears to fulfill exactly romantic aspirations which she had despaired of ever finding in real life. Marú cancels her wedding plans against all family and social considerations, and decides to search for her "double," whom she feels she was predestined to love. Unaware of the young man's ultimate fate (somewhat ambiguous, since his body was never recovered), Marú cannot know that her search is doomed to fail. But perhaps it is just as well, because what she has gained is an accrued belief in the value of her ideals; a faith which might sustain her, and give significance to a life which she could otherwise never accept.

The type of romantic heroine exemplified by Melisa and Marú is repeated in all but two of Salinas' plays. One exception is the previously mentioned *Cain or a Glory of Science,* where the protagonist is the disillusioned inventor of the atomic bomb; the other is a play dealing with the Spanish Civil War, entitled *Los santos (The Saints),* to which I shall later return. In all the other plays, we witness a woman's rebellion against circumstances which are too narrowly defined, against a staid or hypocritical social code, or against materialistic values, as in the case of *Sobre seguro (About Insurance),* a satirical play in which the protagonist is a mother who refuses to cash in a life insurance policy because it seems to her a betrayal of her son's love to benefit materially from his death.

Judit, in the three-act play *Judit y el tirano (Judith and the Tyrant),* expresses a philosophy of life common to all of Salinas' protagonists:

La vida más verdadera hay que vivirla algunas veces con luz de comedia, con palabras de comedia . . . Porque su verdad es tan tremenda que, vista cara a cara, nos aterraría . . . Hay que jugar con ella, . . . hacer nuestra comedia . . . de verdades . . . que se disfrazan de juegos. . . . Vestidas de su fría razón, serían insufribles. Las salvamos fantaseándolas. . . . Y así, entrando en nuestro papel, entramos en la vida verdadera . . . La comedia de las verdades . . . para acabar con el embuste. (pp. 344-45)

(Sometimes, we must face the real truth of life as if we were under stage lights, with words borrowed from a play . . . Because this truth is so awesome that seen face to face it would terrify us. We must play with it, . . . create our own comedy . . . of truths . . . which pass for games. . . . Seen in the light of cold reason, they would be intolerable. . . . Therefore, in assuming our acting role, we will live life as it really is . . . A comedy of truths . . . to end the imposture.)

Judit has attempted to live her life in a role of her choice: that of the heroine of a political cause. But she is an exception;

for most of Salinas' protagonists, the favored escape remains the dream of some unattainable love ideal. Just as with many of Lorca's characters (such as the protagonist of *The Shoemaker's Prodigious Wife*), this escape takes the form of a dream world, a happy shelter where they may for a time enjoy an imaginary freedom.

Most of Salinas' plays dealing with the love theme end on this happy dream of romantic escape, without exploring the eventual consequences. But in a few works, such as *La cabeza de Medusa* (*The Head of Medusa*), and more conclusively, in the three-act allegory entitled *El director* (*The Director*), the inevitable journey from illusion back to reality occurs as the protagonist succumbs to an overwhelming desire to test her dreamed adventure in real life, meeting thereby with disillusionment and despair. The antithetical attraction of dream and reality is seen as a fatal cyclic struggle from which there is no escape, at least within the confines of Salinas' theater.

One more play deserves more than a passing mention, since it reveals something of the author's feelings toward the emotionally charged subject of the Spanish Civil War. This play, *The Saints*, was not included in the volume of *Teatro completo* because, due to its subject matter, it could never have passed the Spanish regime's official censure. The only available text is the version published in the Mexican literary and arts periodical *Cuadernos Americanos* (XIII, No. 3, 1954). Yet, the play is in no way polemical. Although the author's Republican sympathies are obvious, he rises above political considerations to condemn fratricidal hatred on both sides of the conflict. As in the novel, his protest is against man's cruelty to man and the madness of war in general.

The action is situated in a village of New Castile, in the early days of the war. The village's position on the front causes it to change hands repeatedly, thereby allowing the appearance on stage of both rival bands. The scene of action is the cellar of the town's main church, where wooden statues of saints and other liturgical objects and artistic treasures have been hidden against possible iconoclastic rampages.

The play opens as a detachment from a People's Militia has just captured the town. The cellar door is forced, and the wooden statues are almost mistaken for real hiding Fascists and fired upon. Even after they have been identified as part of the church's treasure, some trigger-happy soldiers are ready to use the statues for target practice. One of them, symbolizing blind fanaticism, wants to "execute" the saints as Fascists, or at least as sympathizers, since anything which "reeks of the Church" is automatically suspect. Reason finally prevails, and two soldiers are assigned to sort and catalog the objects as part of the national art treasure. While the two men are busy at their task, a counter-offensive brings the enemy back to the center of town. One of the militiamen escapes, but the other decides to hide among the statues. As he does, covering himself with church ornaments, he is struck by the saints' incredibly human expression of sorrow, especially on the face of one of the Virgins.

The Nationalists decide to use the cellar as a jail for hostages awaiting summary execution. The prisoners are a motley group: a carpenter whose only fault has been to refuse to build a scaffold; a mother who tried to defend her son; a simple-minded peasant, completely innocent but victim of mistaken identity; a prostitute who became a camp follower with the Republican forces, and others. The discussion which ensues among them provides the play's pivotal scene. Every one begins by protesting his innocence, concerned only with the injustice done in his own particular case. But it is clear that the issue is not one of guilt or innocence, since these can change by a capricious turn of fate or circumstances. It is discovered that one of the least conspicuous prisoners is actually a nun. By her status alone, she should have belonged to the opposing side and, branded as an agent of "obscurantism," automatically been rejected by her companions. Yet she too has been accused by the Fascists, on the basis of circumstantial evidence, of having facilitated the escape of some leftists. She did not reveal her true identity nor even bother to defend herself against her accusers.

The incongruity of having a nun for a companion brings the group to the realization that all are united by a common fraternal bond. A new feeling of solidarity is born among the prisoners, who are no longer concerned only with saving their own individual skins. Instead, the nun brings the group around to the idea of an unselfish sacrifice. They will save the militiaman, whose presence is still unsuspected by the enemy, by providing him with some of their own civilian clothes. They themselves will be shot, but he can remain hidden among the statues and escape later.

This feeling of fraternal love is what saves the group. As the prisoners are about to be called to their execution, a miracle occurs. The wooden statues come alive, and it is they who trade clothes with the condemned humans. A few minutes later, they are taken out of the cellar. Shots from the firing squad tell the accused that they have indeed been saved by this supernatural intervention.

The Saints is undoubtedly Salinas' most compelling play. The subject matter itself bring it close to our sensibilities. Moreover, its characters strike one as completely authentic Spanish types, whose personality and language Salinas has so faithfully reproduced. But the play is also well constructed; its fantastic ending does not seem gratuitous because the saints' metamorphosis has been prepared for in the previous scenes. The similarity between this play and *The Incredible Bomb* is obvious, but in this single instance it is the dramatic rendering which seems the most convincing.

Notes and References

Chapter One

1. As quoted by Guillermo de Torre, *Historia de las literaturas de vanguardia* (Madrid, 1965), p. 546.
2. On the poetics of the Generation of 1927, see Biruté Ciplijauskaité, *El poeta y la poesía* (Madrid, 1966), pp. 271-382, especially p. 354.
3. Ricardo Gullón, "La 'generación' poética de 1925," *La invención del '98 y otros ensayos* (Madrid, 1969), pp. 147-48.
4. Dámaso Alonso, "Una generación poética (1920-1936)," *Poetas españoles contemporáneos* (Madrid, 1958), p. 183.
5. On Góngora's influence on the Generation of 1927, see Elsa Dehennin, *La Résurgence de Góngora et la Génération Poétique de 1927* (Paris, 1962), especially the Conclusion, pp. 245-55.
6. Alonso, p. 172.
7. On the contemporary resurgence of the ballad, see Pedro Salinas, "El romancismo y el Siglo XX," *Ensayos de literatura hispánica,* 3rd ed. (Madrid, 1967), pp. 326-59.
8. C. B. Morris, "The Game of Poetry," *A Generation of Spanish Poets, 1920-1936* (Cambridge, 1969), pp. 84-118. Also, Guillermo de Torre, pp. 569-70.
9. Federico García Lorca, "La imagen poética de Don Luis de Góngora," *Obras completas,* 6th ed. (Madrid, 1963), p. 67.
10. Joaquín González Muela, "La poesía de la Generación de 1927," *Spanish Thought and Letters of the Twentieth Century,* edited by Germán Bleiberg and Inman Fox (Nashville, 1966), p. 250.
11. Jorge Guillén, *Language and Poetry* (Cambridge, Mass., 1966), p. 210.
12. Andrew Debicki, *Estudios sobre poesía española contemporánea* (Madrid, 1968), p. 37.

Chapter Two

1. Pedro Salinas, *Poesías completas* (Barcelona, 1971), pp. 785-87.
2. The title of three of these articles is given in Angel del Río, "El poeta Pedro Salinas: vida y obra," *Estudios sobre literatura contemporánea española* (Madrid, 1966), p. 182, n. 2.

3. A complete list of poems published in *Revista de Occidente* appears in Alma de Zubizarreta, *Pedro Salinas: el diálogo creador* (Madrid, 1969), pp. 370-71.

4. *Contemporary Spanish Poetry: Selections from Ten Poets,* Eleanor L. Turnbull, ed. and translator (Baltimore, 1945), pp. 1-35. Includes both Salinas' original Spanish text and its English translation.

5. The first volume appeared in 1922, and the last, Part I of *The World of Guermantes,* in 1931. These translations have been recently reissued by Alianza Editorial (Madrid: Colección "El libro de Bolsillo," Nos. 22, 33, and 40).

6. He lectured on other topics besides literature. For example, in 1958 he delivered a lecture in English on "The Psychology of the Spaniard as Portrayed in Spanish Painting" at the University of Oklahoma.

7. Lowell Dunham, "Don Pedro se nos ha ido," *Books Abroad,* Vol. 26 (Spring, 1952), 155-56. Despite its Spanish title, the article is in English.

8. The following correspondence has been published: "Siete cartas de Pedro Salinas a Jorge Guillén"; "Cartas sudamericanas"; Guillermo de Torre, "Pedro Salinas en mi recuerdo y en sus cartas," all three selections in *Buenos Aires Literaria,* No. 13 (1953). Dámaso Alonso published "España en las cartas de Pedro Salinas," *Insula,* No. 74 (1952), 1 and 5, reprinted in Alonso's *Del siglo de oro a este siglo de siglas* (Madrid, 1962), pp. 154-62. Finally, Alan S. Bell recently published some of Salinas' correspondence with his English translator: "Pedro Salinas en América: su correspondencia con Eleanor Turnbull," *Insula,* No. 307 (1972), 1 and 12-13. The letters to Guillén and Alonso are particularly revealing of Salinas' intimate personality. A complete edition of Salinas' correspondence is in preparation.

9. Vicente Aleixandre, "En casa de Pedro Salinas," *Insula,* No. 127 (1957), 1-2.

10. Jorge Guillén, in his introduction to Pedro Salinas, *Reality and the Poet in Spanish Poetry,* 2d. ed. (Baltimore, 1966), p. xiii.

11. *Ibid.,* p. xiv.

12. See Jorge Guillén, "Poeta y profesor"; Eugenio Florit, "Mi Pedro Salinas"; Marguerite C. Rand, "Pedro Salinas: An Appreciation," and others, in *Hispania,* XXXV (May, 1952), 147-57.

13. Pedro Salinas, *Jorge Manrique o tradición y originalidad* (Buenos Aires, 1947). See Juan Meléndez Valdés, *Poesías,* edición, prólogo y notas de Pedro Salinas (Madrid, 1925).

14. Salinas, "Significación del esperpento o Valle-Inclán, hijo

pródigo del '98," *Literatura española Siglo XX,* 3d. ed. (Madrid, 1970), pp. 86-114.

15. Salinas, *La poesía de Rubén Darío* (Buenos Aires, 1948), p. 51.

16. Salinas, "Don Quijote y la novela," *Ensayos de literatura hispánica,* p. 113.

17. Salinas, *Reality and the Poet . . .* , p. 5.

18. Salinas, "Defensa del lenguaje," *El defensor,* 2d. ed. (Madrid, 1967), p. 305.

19. Salinas, "Defensa de la minoría literaria," *Ibid.,* pp. 220-21.

20. Salinas, "Una metáfora en dos tiempos," *Ensayos de literatura hispánica,* p. 178.

21. Salinas, "El romancismo y el siglo XX," *Ibid.,* p. 351.

22. See the statement by Salinas in Gerardo Diego, *Poesía española contemporánea—Antología* (Madrid, 1934), p. 303.

23. The book, originally published in 1940 by the Johns Hopkins Press, contains lectures given at Johns Hopkins in 1937. This collection, so far, has been published only in an English translation by Edith Helman. The second edition (Baltimore, 1966) contains the valuable Guillén introduction.

24. Elsa Dehennin, *Passion d'Absolu et Tension Expressive dans l'Oeuvre Poétique de Pedro Salinas* (Ghent, 1957), p. 68.

25. Judith Feldbaum, "El trasmundo de la obra poética de Pedro Salinas," *Revista Hispánica Moderna,* XXII (January, 1956), 12-34. Guillermo Díaz-Plaja, *La poesía lírica española* (Barcelona, 1948), p. 418.

26. Carlos Feal Deibe, *La poesía de Pedro Salinas* (Madrid, 1965), p. 17.

27. Dehennin, *Passion d'Absolu . . .* , p. 191.

28. Julian Palley, *La luz no usada—la poesía de Pedro Salinas* (México, 1966), p. 41.

29. *Ibid.,* p. 54.

30. Olga Costa Viva, *Pedro Salinas frente a la realidad* (Madrid, 1969), pp. 23 and 32.

31. Salinas, *Reality and the Poet . . .* , p. 164.

32. de Zubizarreta, p. 20.

33. del Río, p. 230.

34. Jorge Guillén, *Cántico,* first complete ed. (Buenos Aires, 1950), p. 523.

35. Salinas, *Reality and the Poet . . .* , p. 63.

Chapter Three

1. The latest edition of Salinas' P.C. (*Poesías completas*), edited by Soledad Salinas de Marichal (Barcelona, 1971), contains an addi-

tional book of poetry entitled *Largo lamento* (*Long Lament*), as
well as isolated, hitherto unpublished poems. The history of *Largo
lamento* is rather complicated. Parts of it had already been published
by Juan Marichal (Milan, 1958) in two small volumes under the
title *Volverse sombra y otros poemas* (*To Turn to Shadow and
Other Poems*) and *Amor, mundo en peligro* (*Love, A World in Peril*).
To the poems contained in those two books Soledad Salinas has now
added eleven unpublished poems found among the poet's papers
after his death, poems obviously belonging to the same cycle.

Most of the poems in *Long Lament* seem to belong to the love
cycle period and were probably written in 1937-1938. Originally, it
seems that Salinas did intend to publish them in one volume, but
then changed his mind. As Soledad Salinas puts it, the poet "scattered" his manuscript: *desglosó el manuscrito original de "Largo
lamento" en poemas y textos aislados* (PC, p. 45). Some isolated
poems were published in periodicals, and two groups, "Angel extraviado" and "Entretiempo romántico" later were incorporated in *All
Things Made Clearer,* as we shall see. In his introduction to *To Turn
to Shadow,* Juan Marichal tells us (p. 16) that he found this half
of the apparently forgotten manuscript in a drawer of Salinas' desk
at Johns Hopkins. Questioned about these yellowing pages, Salinas
replied that these poems were of no use to him. It seems clear that
he no longer intended to publish them.

The poems of *Long Lament,* although they are love poems, are
quite different in tone, more personal and, in some cases, written
in a conversational style very unlike that of *The Voice Owed to You*
or *Love's Reason.* Most important, they reflect entirely different
feelings from the basic optimism which transpires in the two main
volumes. It is probably for this reason that Salinas finally decided
against publishing them. Clearly, the logical sequence to *Love's
Reason* is, as we shall see, *The Contemplated Sea.* For this reason,
I have decided not to offer a critical discussion of the poems of
Long Lament. A clear idea of their content can be gotten, however,
from the two sections which are now parts of *All Things Made
Clearer* and with which I shall deal in Chapter 5.

2. According to Jorge Guillén, in his introduction to Salinas'
Reality and the Poet . . . , p. xxiii.

3. *Lunes del Imparcial,* January 7, 1918.

4. *Poesías completas* (Barcelona, 1971), as indicated in note 1
above. All quoted texts and page numbers refer to this latest edition.

5. Bracketed ellipses are mine.

6. Antonio Machado, *Poesías completas,* 8th ed. (Madrid, 1959),
p. 164.

7. Angel del Río, *op. cit.*, pp. 193-94.

8. *Ibid.*, p. 199.

9. Julian Palley gives a different interpretation of this poem in keeping with his view of Salinas' obsession with nothingness: in *The Poem Itself*, ed. by Stanley Burnshaw (New York, 1962), pp. 202-3.

10. Elsa Dehennin, *Passion d'Absolu . . .*, p. 31.

11. Translations by Alice Jane McVan, *Translations from Hispanic Poets* (New York, 1938), p. 151.

12. On the symbolism of water, see Chapter 4, p. 82.

Chapter Four

1. The poem is from *Sobre los ángeles (Concerning the Angels)*, in Rafael Alberti, *Obras completas* (Buenos Aires, 1961), p. 278.

2. The revised edition of *Poesías completas* has reestablished the clear separation between each poem, which was not always distinguishable in the 1955 edition. In addition, each poem is now numbered in the Table of Contents for easier reference.

3. Stephen Gilman, "The Proem to *'La voz a ti debida,'* " *Modern Language Quarterly*, XXIII (1963), 353.

4. Joaquín González Muela, ed., *La voz a ti debida y Razón de amor*, by Pedro Salinas (Madrid, 1969), p. 16.

5. Leo Spitzer, "El conceptismo interior de Pedro Salinas," *Revista Hispánica Moderna*, VII (1941), 37.

6. Pierre Darmangeat, *Pedro Salinas et "La voz a ti debida"* (Paris, 1956), p. 40.

7. Guillermo Díaz-Plaja, *La poesía lírica española* (Barcelona, 1948), pp. 418-19.

8. C. B. Morris, *A Generation of Spanish Poets* (Chap. 1, note 8), p. 167.

9. Judith Feldbaum, Elsa Dehennin, Stephen Gilman, Carlos Feal Deibe, Alma de Zubizarreta, and Olga Costa Viva, among others, do not question the fact that Pedro Salinas addressed himself to a real woman. Judith Feldbaum ("El trasmundo de la obra poética de Pedro Salinas," *Revista Hispánica Moderna*, XXII, 25) was, I believe, the first critic to see the narrative structure of the poem as the "story" of a love affair: *Una historia de amor con el enamoramiento repentino, la alegría del amor logrado, la angustia de dudas y ausencias . . .*

10. Jorge Guillén, introduction to Salinas' *Reality and the Poet . . .*, p. xxvii.

11. This edition included eleven poems of *La voz a ti debida*; Nos. 17, 20, 8, 14, 15, 19, 65, 45, 64, and 66 of the definitive edition, in that order.

12. Gilman, pp. 357-58.

13. The only edition that provides a verse count is that of Joaquín González Muela. I have indented these verse numbers in the Spanish quotes for easier reference.

14. González Muela, p. 70 n.

15. We can see that the first three parts correspond to three aspects of love in the order set forth in the book's epigraph.

16. Palley, *La luz no usada*... (Chap. II, n. 20), p. 61.

17. Feal Deibe, *La poesía de Pedro Salinas* (Chap. II, n. 18), p. 76.

18. See the very complete analysis of this poem given by Olga Costa Viva, *Pedro Salinas frente a la realidad* (Chap. II, n. 22), pp. 53-63.

19. The same motif is developed again, more extensively, in "Fin del mundo" (End of the World"), No. 49 of *Love's Reason*.

20. The allusion is made even more specific in the first poem of *Love's Reason*, verses 24-30, p. 335.

21. Morris, p. 164.

22. Guillén, introduction to Salinas' *Reality and the Poet*, p. xxix.

23. The word *razón* can mean both "reasoning" and "reason why."

24. After No. 32, there are no longer any "negative" poems.

25. Feal Deibe (p. 202) sees love as the key to salvation in *Love's Reason*. I subscribe fully to this view. Joaquín González Muela claims to disagree (pp. 38 and 185 n.), and suggests that salvation will be attained through the poetic "corpus" which provides a means to immortality. We have seen that both solutions are really interrelated and equally valid.

26. Salinas' view of the sea comes very close to that so often expressed in the poetry of Juan Ramón Jiménez.

27. Other examples can be found. In his use of *enjambement*, Fray Luis goes so far as to ending a verse in midword, as in his Ode "La vida retirada" ("The Withdrawn Life"): ... *Y mientras miserable-/ mente se están los otros abrazando* ... (and while so miserab-/ ly others are embracing ...).

28. Jacques Maritain, *Creative Intuition in Art and Poetry* (New York, 1953), p. 321.

29. Feal Deibe, p. 184.

Chapter Five

1. Alma de Zubizarreta, *Pedro Salinas: el diálogo creador* (Chap. II, note 24), pp. 92, 96 n., 207.

2. Juan Marichal, "Pedro Salinas: La voz a la confidencia debida," *Revista de Occidente*, No. 26 (May, 1965), 154-70.

3. See the development of these ideas in Pierre Teilhard de Chardin, *Le Phénomène Humain* (Paris, 1949).

4. Marichal, p. 156.

5. I would like to suggest once more that Salinas' development might have been inspired at an early date by the ideas of Ortega y Gasset. As early as 1923, in *El tema de nuestro tiempo* (*The Theme of our Time*), Ortega made the following statement: "Life is the cosmic realization of altruism and exists solely as a perpetual emigration of the vital Ego in the direction of the Non-Self." (The quote is from *The Modern Theme*, trans. by James Cleugh, 2d ed. [New York, 1961], p. 72.) This is essentially Salinas' mature position. It took the experience described in *The Voice Owed to You* to prepare him emotionally to accept this basically altruistic concept of individual fulfillment.

6. Gustavo Correa, "El contemplado," *Hispania*, XXXV (May, 1952), 139.

7. Andrew Debicki, *Estudios sobre poesía* . . . (Chap. I, note 12), p. 95.

8. On the other end, Jorge Guillén, in his introduction to the revised edition of Salinas' *Complete Poems*, compares this poem to Valéry's "Le Cimetière Marin," p. 33.

9. Pedro Salinas, *Zero*, trans. by Eleanor Turnbull (Baltimore, 1947).

10. Federico García Lorca, "Vuelta de paseo," *Obras completas*, 6th ed. (Madrid, 1963), p. 471.

11. These are the poems which were originally to be included in *Long Lament*.

12. Such as Alberti's "Tres recuerdos del cielo" (see Chap. 4, n. 1) and Aleixandre's "El vals" from *Espadas como labios*. See Vicente Aleixandre, *Poesías completas* (Madrid, 1960), p. 234.

13. Debicki, p. 88.

Chapter Six

1. "Siete cartas de Pedro Salinas a Jorge Guillén," *Buenos Aires Literaria*, No. 13 (1953), 29.

2. *El defensor*, 2d. ed. (Madrid, 1967), p. 15. This and subsequent page numbers refer to this edition.

3. *Ibid.*, p. 56.

4. *Ibid.*, p. 298.

5. *Ibid.*, pp. 246-47.

6. Northrop Frye, *The Critical Path* (Bloomington, Indiana, 1971), p. 36.

7. *El defensor*, p. 29.

8. *Ibid.*, p. 77.

9. José Manual Blecua, "Una charla con Pedro Salinas," *Insula,* No. 70 (Octubre, 1951), 6.

10. Miguel Artola, "Denuncia del tiempo futuro," *Cuadernos Hispanoamericanos,* XXIV (1955), 150-57; Ricardo Gullón, "Pedro Salinas, novelista," *Insula,* No. 71 (Noviembre, 1951), 3.

11. Salinas, *La bomba increíble,* 2a. edición (Buenos Aires, 1959). Subsequent page numbers also refer to this edition.

12. Gullón, 3.

13. Pedro Salinas, *El desnudo impecable y otras narraciones* (Mexico, 1951). All page numbers refer to this edition.

14. Edith Helman sees this as the central theme of the book. See her review entitled "The Innocent and the Guilty," *Hispania,* XXXV, No. 2 (1952), 151-52.

15. "Siete cartas de Pedro Salinas a Jorge Guillén," pp. 32-33 and Guillermo de Torre, "Pedro Salinas en mi recuerdo y en sus cartas," p. 93. See also Juan Marichal's introduction to Pedro Salinas, *Teatro completo* (Madrid, 1957), pp. 11-13.

16. Dámaso Alonso, "Con Pedro Salinas," *Poetas españoles contemporáneos,* pp. 196-98.

17. Performances of plays by Salinas took place at the University of Puerto Rico in December, 1971, as part of a commemoration of the twentieth anniversary of the poet's death: Three plays were presented: *Judit y el tirano* (*Judith and the Tyrant*), *Ella y sus fuentes* (*She and Her Sources*), and *El chantajista* (*The Blackmailer*).

18. Edith Helman, "Verdad y fantasia en el teatro de Pedro Salinas," *Buenos Aires Literaria,* No. 13 (1953), 69-78; Mario Maurín, "Temas y variaciones en el teatro de Pedro Salinas," *Insula,* No. 104 (1954), 1 and 3; José Rodríguez Richart, "Sobre el teatro de Pedro Salinas," *Boletín de la Biblioteca Menéndez y Pelayo,* XXVI (1960), 397-427.

19. Helman, "Verdad y fantasia . . . ," p. 72.

20. This and subsequent page numbers refer to *Teatro completo.*

21. Maurín, 3.

Selected Bibliography

The bibliography on Salinas is extensive. In my selection of secondary sources, I have included all book-length studies, but only those articles which are mentioned in the notes. The most complete bibliography is found in Alma de Zubizarretta, *Pedro Salinas: el diálogo creador*. Other useful bibliographies appear in *Revista Hispánica Moderna*, VII (1941), and in Julian Palley, *La luz no usada, poesía de Pedro Salinas*.

PRIMARY SOURCES

1. Books of Verse

Presagios (Madrid: Biblioteca de Indice, 1923).
Seguro azar (Madrid: Revista de Occidente, 1929).
Fábula y signo (Madrid: Plutarco, 1931).
Amor en vilo (Madrid: La Tentative Poética, 1933).
La voz a ti debida (Madrid: Los Cuatro Vientos, 1933).
Razón de amor (Madrid: Cruz y Raya, 1936).
Poesía junta (Buenos Aires: Losada, 1942).
El contemplado (mar, poema): tema con variaciones (México: Stylo, 1946).
Todo más claro y otros poemas (Buenos Aires: Losada, 1949).
Poemas escogidos, Prologue by Jorge Guillén (Buenos Aires: Espasa-Calpe [Austral], 1953).
Confianza, poemas inéditos, Ed. Juan Marichal, prologue by Jorge Guillén (Madrid: Aguilar, 1955).
Poesías completas, Ed. Juan Marichal (Madrid: Aguilar, 1955).
Amor, mundo en peligro (poema) (Milan: Scheiwiller, 1957).
Volverse sombra y otros poemas, Ed. and prologue by Juan Marichal (Milan: Scheiwiller, 1957).
La voz a ti debida y Razón de amor. Critical edition by Joaquín González Muela (Madrid: Castalia, 1969).
Poesía. Anthology edited by Julio Cortázar (Madrid: Alianza, 1971).
Poesías completas. Second augmented edition, ed. Soledad Salinas de Marichal, prologue by Jorge Guillén (Barcelona: Barral, 1971).

2. Narrative Prose and Theater

Víspera del gozo (Madrid: Revista de Occidente, 1926).

La bomba increíble (Buenos Aires: Sudamericana, 1950; second edition, 1959).

El desnudo impecable y otras narraciones (México: Tezontle, 1951).

Teatro: "La cabeza de Medusa," "La estratoesfera," "La isla del tesoro" (Madrid: Insula, 1952).

"Los santos," *Cuadernos Americanos* (Mexico), XIII, No. 3 (1954).

Teatro completo. Ed. Juan Marichal (Madrid: Aguilar, 1957).

3. Essays and Literary Criticism (excluding critical editions)

Reality and the Poet in Spanish Poetry (Baltimore: The Johns Hopkins Press, 1940; second edition, prologue by Jorge Guillén, 1960).

Literatura española siglo XX (México: Séneca, 1941; second augmented edition, 1949; third edition [Madrid: Alianza], 1969).

La poesía de Rubén Darío (México: Séneca, 1946).

Jorge Manrique, o tradición y originalidad (Buenos Aires: Sudamericana, 1949; second edition, 1949; third edition [Madrid: Alianza], 1962).

El defensor (Bogotá: Universidad Mayor, 1948; second edition, ed. and prologue by Juan Marichal [Madrid: Alianza], 1967).

Ensayos de literatura hispánica (Del "Cantar de Mio Cid" a García Lorca). Ed. and prologue, Juan Marichal (Madrid: Aguilar, 1958).

La responsabilidad del escritor y otros ensayos. Ed. and prologue, Juan Marichal (Barcelona: Seix Barral, 1961).

1. English Translations of Works by Salinas

"Raving Lament of the Poplar and the Cypress" ("Delirios del chopo y el ciprés," *Víspera del gozo*). Transl. by V. Llona, *The European Caravan.* Ed. Samuel Putnam (New York: Brewer, Warren, and Putnam, 1931).

"Walls, unbroken rise" ("Murallas intactas," *Presagios*, 28). Transl. by Anne S. Durand, *Translations from Hispanic Poets* (New York: The Hispanic Society of America, 1938), pp. 148-49.

"Escorial II" ("Escorial II," *Fábula y signo*). Transl. by Alice Jane McVan, *Translations from Hispanic Poets* (New York: Hispanic Society of America, 1938), pp. 150-51.

Lost Angel and Other Poems. Selections from *Todo más claro.* Transl. by Eleanor L. Turnbull (Baltimore: The Johns Hopkins Press, 1938).

"Three Poems": "If the voice were perceived with the eyes ..." ("Si la voz se sintiera con los ojos"); "Now I love you" ("Ahora te quiero"); "I am so sure of your presence" ("Tan convencido estoy de tu presencia"). All three from *Razón de amor*. Transl. by Eleanor L. Turnbull, *Poet Lore*, XLV (Spring, 1939), 220-25.

"Trilling of bird song" ("Entre el trino y el pájaro," *Razón de amor*); "The Faithless Friend" ("La falsa compañera," *Largo lamento*), *Bread Loaf Anthology* (Middlebury: Middlebury College Press, 1939).

Truth of Two and Other Poems (*La voz a ti debida* and *Razón de amor*). Transl. by Eleanor L. Turnbull (Baltimore: The Johns Hopkins Press, 1940).

"Lost Angel" ("Angel extraviado," *Todo más claro*); "The Faithless Friend" ("La falsa compañera," *Largo lamento*); "This One" ("Esta," *Confianza*). Transl. by Eleanor L. Turnbull, *Contemporary Poetry*, V (Spring, 1945).

"Soil. Nothing More" ("Suelo. Nada más," *Presagios*); "How gently you rock my child to sleep" ("¡Cómo me meces al niño!" *Presagios*); "On dry land" ("En la tierra seca," *Presagios*); "I see you not, though well I know ..." ("No te veo. Bien sé ...," *Presagios*); "The Shore" ("Orilla," *Seguro azar*); "His Triumph" ("Triunfo nuevo," *Seguro azar*); "Distant Sea" ("Mar distante," *Fábula y signo*); "How many lost things there were ..." ("¡Ay, cuántas cosas perdidas!" *La voz a ti debida*); "Not in palaces of marble" ("No en palacios de mármol," *La voz a ti debida*); "Do you not hear how they ask for reality?" ("¿Las oyes como piden realidades?" *La voz a ti debida*); "To think of you tonight" ("Pensar en ti esta noche," *Razón de amor*); "If the voice were perceived with the eyes ..." ("Si la voz se sintiera con los ojos," *Razón de amor*); "Swimmer of night, swimmer between ..." ("Nadador de noche, nadadora ...," *Razón de amor*); "I am so sure that your presence ..." ("Tan convencido estoy ...," *Razón de amor*); "Tell me, do you remember? ..." ("Di ¿te acuerdas de los sueños ...," *Razón de amor*); "Truth of Two" ("Verdad de dos," *Razón de amor*), in *Contemporary Spanish Poetry: Selections from Ten Poets*. Transl. by Eleanor L. Turnbull (Baltimore: The Johns Hopkins Press, 1945).

Zero. Transl. by Eleanor L. Turnbull (Baltimore: The Johns Hopkins Press, 1947).

"Is it the bird, or birds?" ("¿El pájaro, los pájaros?" *Confianza*). Transl. by Eleanor L. Turnbull, *The Hopkins Review* (Spring, 1948), p. 174. "The Stairway at Night (A Jocular Poem)" ("La

escalera de noche [burla]"), in *Poesías completas*, p. 797. Transl.
by Eleanor L. Turnbull, *The Hopkins Review* (Winter, 1949),
p. 237.

Sea of San Juan: A Contemplation (*El contemplado*). Transl. by
Eleanor L. Turnbull (Boston: Bruce Humphries, 1950).
"I don't see you, I know well" ("No te veo, vien sé," *Presagios*),
transl. by Julian Palley; "Deaths" ("Muertes," *Fábula y signo*),
transl. by Eugenio Florit; "To think of you tonight" ("Pensar
en ti esta noche," *Razón de amor*), transl. by Eugenio Florit;
"The Poem" ("El poema," *Todo más claro*), transl. by Eugenio
Florit, in *The Poem Itself*. Ed. Stanley Burnshaw (New York:
The World Publishing Co., 1960).

2. Ultraism and the Generation of 1927

ALBERTI, RAFAEL. *Obras completas* (Buenos Aires: Losada, 1961).

ALEIXANDRE, VICENTE. *Poesías completas* (Madrid: Aguilar, 1960).

ALONSO, DAMASO. "Una generación poética (1920-1936)," *Poetas
españoles contemporáneos* (Madrid: Gredos, 1958), pp. 167-92.
One of the best introductions to the group, with arguments in
favor of considering it as a true literary "generation."

CANO, JOSE LUIS. *La poesía de la generación del '27* (Madrid:
Guadarrama, 1970). Contains a short introductory chapter on
the group, followed by studies on individual poets.

CIPLIJAUSKAITE, BIRUTE. *El poeta y la poesía* (Madrid: Insula, 1966).
See Chapter Six on the aesthetics of the Generation of 1927.

CIRRE, JOSE FRANCISCO. *Forma y espíritu de una lírica española
(1920-1935)*, (México: Gráfica Panamericana, 1950). A good
general study on the poetry, themes, and evolution of this
generation.

DEBICKI, ANDREW. *Estudios sobre poesía española contemporánea:
la generación de 1924-1925* (Madrid: Gredos, 1968). Contains
an excellent introductory chapter on the group as a whole, the
principal themes found in its poetry, and its evolution.

DEHENNIN, ELSA. *La Résurgence de Góngora et la Génération
Poétique de 1927* (Paris: Didier, 1962). A good study on
Góngora's influence on the group.

DIEGO, GERARDO. *Poesía española contemporánea* (antología), (Madrid: Signo, 1934). Includes selections by most of the poets of
the Generation of 1927, with short biographical notes and a
statement by each poet on his aesthetics.

GARCIA LORCA, FEDERICO. *Obras completas*, 6th ed. (Madrid: Aguilar,
1963). See Lorca's essay on Góngora.

GONZALEZ MUELA, JOAQUIN. *El lenguaje poético de la generación Guillén-Lorca* (Madrid: Insula, 1954). On the stylistic characteristics of the poetry of the Generation of 1927.

————. "La poesía de la Generación de 1927," in *Spanish Thought and Letters of the Twentieth Century*. Ed. G. Bleiberg and E. I. Fox (Nashville: Vanderbilt University Press, 1966). On the aesthetics, themes, and evolution of this group.

GUILLEN, JORGE. *Language and Poetry* (Cambridge: Harvard University Press, 1966). The last chapter is on the Generation of 1927 viewed as a cohesive group.

GULLON, RICARDO. "La 'generación' poética de 1925," *La invención del '98 y otros ensayos* (Madrid: Gredos, 1969). Speculates on the existence of the group as a true literary "generation."

MORRIS, C. B. *A Generation of Spanish Poets, 1920-1936* (Cambridge: University Press, 1969). The only general study written in English on the poetry of the Generation of 1927. Makes some rather sweeping generalizations and overemphasizes the "poetry as game" phase of the latter group.

TORRE, GUILLERMO DE. "Contemporary Spanish Poetry," *The Texas Quarterly: Special Issue: Image of Spain*, IV, No. 1 (1961), 55-78. A useful guide to general trends in Spanish poetry, including Ultraism and the Generation of 1927.

————. *Historia de las literaturas de vanguardia* (Madrid: Guadarrama, 1965). See Chapter Seven, on Ultraism.

VIDELA, GLORIA. *El ultraísmo: estudios sobre movimientos de vanguardia en España* (Madrid: Gredos, 1963). The best study on Ultraism and its influence.

3. Critical and Bio-biographical Studies on Salinas

ALEIXANDRE, VICENTE. "En casa de Pedro Salinas," *Insula*, No. 127 (1957), 1 and 2. Personal reminiscences.

ALONSO, DAMASO. "Con Pedro Salinas," *Clavileño*, No. 11 (1951). Reprinted in Alonso's *Poetas españoles contemporáneos* (Madrid: Gredos, 1958). Personal reminiscences of his visit to the United States in 1951.

————. "España en las cartas de Pedro Salinas," *Insula*, No. 74 (1952), 1 and 5. Reprinted in Alonso's *Del siglo de oro a este siglo de siglas* (Madrid: Gredos, 1962). Salinas' letters to Alonso during the five-year period preceding his death, and Alonso's personal reminiscences.

APARICIO, FRANCISCO. "Pedro Salinas y 'La bomba increíble,' " *Razón y Fe*, CXLV (1952), 184-90. Extensive review of Salinas' novel.

ARTOLA, MIGUEL. "Denuncia del tiempo futuro," *Cuadernos Hispano-americanos*, XXIV (1955), 150-57. Considers Salinas' novel along with other fictional anticipations of a futuristic world in works by Orwell, Huxley, Koestler, Doutreligne, and Zamyatin.

BAADER, HORST. *Pedro Salinas. Studien zu seinem dichterischen und kritischen Werk* (Cologne: Koln Romanitische Arbeiten, 1955). An important study of Salinas' Thought System. Good chapter on style in *The Contemplated Sea*.

BELL, ALAN S. "Pedro Salinas en América: su corespondencia con Eleanor Turnbull," *Insula*, No. 307 (1972), 1 and 12-13. Salinas' correspondence with his English translator.

BERBENNI, GINO. *La poesia di Pedro Salinas* (Padua: Rebellato, 1967). A mediocre introductory study on Salinas.

BLECUA, JOSE MANUEL. "Una charla con Pedro Salinas," *Insula*, No. 70 (1951), 2, 3, and 6. An interview with Salinas at Middlebury, in 1951. Good personal profile of the poet.

CANITO, ENRIQUE. "Pedro Salinas, profesor en Sevilla," *Insula*, No. 74 (1952), 5. Reminiscences by a former student of Salinas in Seville.

CANO, JOSE LUIS. "Las narraciones de un poeta," *Insula*, No. 74 (1952), 6-7. Review of *The Impeccable Nude and Other Stories*.

CORREA, GUSTAVO. "El contemplado," *Hispania*, XXXV, No. 2 (1952), 137-42. On the imagery and structure of *The Contemplated Sea*.

COSTA VIVA, OLGA. *Pedro Salinas frente a la realidad* (Madrid: Alfaguara, 1969). A good general study of the poetry, following the critical guidelines set by Salinas in *Reality and the Poet in Spanish Poetry*.

DARMANGEAT, PIERRE. *Pedro Salinas, et "La voz a ti debida"* (Paris: Librairie des Editions Espagnoles, 1955). General study of the love cycle seen as "conceptual."

DEBICKI, ANDREW. "La visión de la realidad en la poesía como tema: tres libros de Salinas," *Estudios sobre poesía española contemporánea* (Madrid: Gredos, 1968). The first essay on the view of reality in Salinas' first three books, and the second on the function of poetry as a theme in Salinas' late poetry.

DEHENNIN, ELSA. *Passion d'Absolu et Tension Expressive dans l'Oeuvre Poétique de Pedro Salinas* (Ghent: Romanica Gandensia, 1957). One of the main studies supporting the thesis of Salinas' basic idealism. Good stylistic analysis of *The Voice Owed to You* and *The Contemplated Sea*.

DIAZ-PLAJA, GUILLERMO. *La poesía lírica española* (Barcelona: Plenitud, 1948). Includes a short discussion of Salinas' alleged Neoplatonism, among remarks on the Generation of 1927 as a whole.

DUNHAM, LOWELL. "Don Pedro se nos ha ido," *Books Abroad,* XXVII (Spring, 1952), 155-56. Eulogy and reminiscences; Salinas' personality and his activities in his last years.

FEAL DEIBE, CARLOS. *La poesía de Pedro Salinas* (Madrid: Gredos, 1965). A major, primarily stylistic, study.

FELDBAUM, JUDITH. "El trasmundo en la obra poética de Pedro Salinas," *Revista Hispánica Moderna,* XXII, No. 1 (1956), 12-34. An excellent study on the evolution of Salinas' attitude toward reality.

GILMAN, STEPHEN. "The Proem to 'La voz a ti debida,' " *Modern Language Quarterly,* XXIII (1963), 353-59. On the structure of *The Voice Owed to You* and its debt to Bécquer's *Rimas.*

GUILLEN, JORGE. "Poesía de Pedro Salinas," *Buenos Aires Literaria,* No. 13 (1953), 41-54.

GULLON, RICARDO. "Pedro Salinas, novelista," *Insula,* No. 71 (1951), 3. Extensive review of Salinas' novel.

HELMAN, EDITH. "The Innocent and the Guilty," *Hispania,* XXXV, No. 2 (1952), 151-52. Review of *The Impeccable Nude and Other Stories.*

—————. "Verdad y fantasía en el teatro de Pedro Salinas," *Buenos Aires Literaria,* No. 13 (1953), 69-78. General thematic study on Salinas' theater, with emphasis on the three plays included in *Teatro* (1952).

MARICHAL, JUAN. "Pedro Salinas y los valores humanos," *Cuadernos del Congreso por la Libertad de la Cultura,* No. 21 (1956), 48-54. Reprinted in *La voluntad del estilo* (Barcelona: Seix Barral, 1957), and as the prologue to Pedro Salinas, *Ensayos de literatura hispánica.* On Salinas' approach to literary criticism.

—————. "Pedro Salinas: la voz a la confidencia debida," *Revista de Occidente,* 2a. época, No. 26 (1965), 154-70. A major essay on the evolution of Salinas' thought.

MAURIN, MARIO. "Temas y variaciones en el teatro de Pedro Salinas," *Insula,* No. 104 (1954), 1 and 3. A thematic study of Salinas' theater. Comparison with Jean Giraudoux.

MORRIS, C. B. *A Generation of Spanish Poets, 1920-1936* (Cambridge: Cambridge University Press, 1969). Chapter One on Salinas' early poetry, and Four on the poetry of the love cycle.

PALLEY, JULIAN. *La luz no usada: la poesía de Pedro Salinas* (México: Studium, 1966). A major study, originally a doctoral dissertation entitled "The Idea of Nothingness in the Poetry of Pedro Salinas" (University of New Mexico, 1957).

RAMIREZ DE ARELLANO, DIANA. *Caminos de la creación poética de*

Pedro Salinas (Madrid: Biblioteca Aristarco, 1956). A general study.

Rio, Angel del. "El poeta Pedro Salinas: vida y obra," *Revista Hispánica Moderna,* VII (1941), 1-32. Reprinted in *Estudios sobre literatura contemporánea española* (Madrid: Gredos, 1966). An early and very important general study. Biography, critical analysis, and evaluation.

Rodriguez Monegal, Emir. "La obra en prosa de Salinas," *Número* (Montevideo), IX, No. 18 (1952), 66-92. A major study on Salinas' literary criticism and narrative prose.

Rodriguez Richart. Jose. "Sobre el teatro de Pedro Salinas," *Boletín de la Biblioteca Menéndez y Pelayo,* XXVI (1960), 397-427. A good general study on Salinas' theater.

Spitzer, Leo. "El conceptismo interior de Pedro Salinas," *Revista Hispanica Moderna,* VII (1941), 33-69. The first important (and controversial) study on *The Voice Owed to You.* Sustains the view of Salinas' love poetry as an exercise in self-knowledge deemphasizing the woman's role. Good stylistic analysis.

Torre, Guillermo de. "Pedro Salinas en mi recuerdo y en sus cartas," *Buenos Aires Literaria,* No. 13 (1953), 86-96. Quotes from Salinas, and personal reminiscences.

Zubizarreta, Alma de. *Pedro Salinas: el diálogo creador.* Prologue by Jorge Guillén (Madrid: Gredos, 1969). An important thematic and stylistic study. Best bibliography.

4. Special Issues of Journals Dedicated to Salinas

Asomante (Puerto Rico), No. 2 (1952). Primarily eulogies and personal reminiscences.

Buenos Aires Literaria, II, No. 13 (1953). Critical studies, correspondence, personal reminiscences, many photographs, good bibliography. A very important issue.

Insula, No. 74 (1952). Critical studies, reviews, bibliography.

Insula, Nos. 300-301 (1971). Commemorating twentieth anniversary of the poet's death. Critical studies, unpublished poems.

Hispania, XXXV, No. 2 (1952). Many important critical studies, reviews, personal recollections. One of the three best bibliographies.

Número (Montevideo), IV, No. 18 (1953). Critical studies, one play.

Revista Hispánica Moderna, VII (1941). Many important studies. Reprinted as a monograph, *Pedro Salinas* (New York: The Hispanic Society of America, 1941).

5.   Other References for General Background

Frye, Northrop. *The Critical Path* (Bloomington: Indiana University Press, 1971).

Machado, Antonio. *Poesías completas,* 8th ed. (Madrid: Aguilar [Austral], 1959).

Maritain, Jacques. *Creative Intuition in Art and Poetry* (Washington: Pantheon Books, 1953).

Ortega y Gasset, Jose. *The Modern Theme,* 2d ed., transl. by James Cleugh (New York: Harper, 1961).

Teilhard de Chardin, Pierre. *Le Phénomène Humain* (Paris: Seuil, 1949).

Index

The following abbreviations are used in references to Salinas' works: *Pres* (*Presagios*), *Visp* (*Víspera del gozo*), *Azar* (*Seguro azar*), *Fab* (*Fábula y signo*), *Voz* (*La voz a ti debida*), *Raz* (*Razón de amor*), *Cont* (*El contemplado*), *Todo* (*Todo más claro*), *Conf* (*Confianza*), *Bomba* (*La bomba increíble*), *Def* (*El defensor*), *Desn* (*El desnudo impecable*).

175